Cybersecurity guide

The Ultimate Handbook for Middles

William Johanson

© **Copyright 2023 - All rights reserved.**

The contents of this book may not be reproduced, duplicated or transmitted without direct written permission from the author.

Under no circumstances will any legal responsibility or blame be held against the publisher for any reparation, damages, or monetary loss due to the information herein, either directly or indirectly.

Legal Notice:
This book is copyright protected. This is only for personal use. You cannot amend, dis-tribute, sell, use, quote or paraphrase any part or the content within this book without the consent of the author.

Disclaimer Notice:
Please note the information contained within this document is for educational and entertainment purposes only. Every attempt has been made to provide accurate, up to date and reliable complete information. Readers acknowledge that the author is not engaging in the rendering of legal, financial, medical or professional advice. The content of this book has been derived from various sources. Please consult a licensed professional before attempting any techniques outlined in this book.

By reading this document, the reader agrees that under no circumstances is the author responsible for any losses, direct or indirect, which are incurred as a result of the use of information contained within this document.

Table Of Contents

Introduction 4

Chapter One: Understanding Cyber Threats 7

Chapter Two: Building a Solid Foundation 24

Chapter Three: Advanced Endpoint Protection 47

Chapter Four: Secure Coding Practices 69

Chapter Five: Threat Hunting Strategies 88

Chapter Six: Network Security Beyond Basics 102

Chapter Seven: Advanced Cryptography 120

Chapter Eight: Cloud Security Best Practices 137

Chapter Nine: Incident Response and Cyber Forensics 154

Chapter Ten: Securing IoT Devices 170

Chapter Eleven: Emerging Technologies and Future Trends 185

Conclusions 201

Introduction

Welcome to "Cybersecurity Guide: The Ultimate Handbook for Middles." In the rapidly changing landscape of digital threats, building a strong defense is crucial. As an intermediate specialist, you are at a crucial point, ready to enhance your expertise.

The digital age has brought us unparalleled connectivity and convenience, but it has also brought more sophisticated cyber threats. In this dynamic environment, where the stakes are high and the adversaries unrelenting, having an advanced and proactive cybersecurity approach is vital.

This handbook stands out from the abundance of cybersecurity literature. It is a carefully crafted resource tailored for individuals at the intermediate level, aiming to move beyond the basics and delve into the complexities of modern cybersecurity challenges.

Visualize yourself not just as a defender of digital assets but as a strategist skilled at navigating the complexities of cyber threats. Our aim is to provide you with the knowledge and skills needed to understand the intricacies of today's cybersecurity challenges confidently.

The initial chapters introduce you to the current threat landscape. We explore recent cyber attacks, breaking down their methodologies and examining the anatomy of threat vectors. This foundation provides the context necessary to understand the advanced strategies we will discuss later.

Building on this, the handbook guides you through the essentials of cybersecurity, reinforcing foundational principles and exploring their application in the contemporary digital ecosystem. From secure coding practices to robust endpoint protection, each topic is discussed with a focus on practicality and real-world relevance.

A crucial chapter addresses the aspect of threat hunting, a proactive approach that empowers you to identify and neutralize potential threats before they escalate. We delve into the world of threat intelligence, teaching you how to use actionable insights to stay ahead of adversaries.

Network security, often seen as a basic tenet, is revisited with an advanced lens. The discussions go beyond traditional configurations, exploring the implementation of intrusion detection and prevention systems and the art of segmentation for enhanced security.

Cryptographic protocols and algorithms take center stage as we unravel the secure communication landscape. From secure key management to the use of cryptography in blockchain technology, we simplify these concepts, empowering you to implement robust cryptographic measures.

As cloud computing becomes more common, a dedicated section focuses on securing cloud environments. We address the unique challenges presented by cloud configurations, concentrating on identity and access management and continuous monitoring for enhanced security.

The latter chapters explore incident response and cyber forensics, equipping you with the skills needed to handle and learn from security incidents. The complexities of securing IoT devices are clarified, followed by a forward-looking exploration of emerging technologies and future trends in cybersecurity.

This handbook is not just a static compilation of information but a dynamic guide that encourages continuous improvement. As you progress through these pages, imagine yourself not just as a cybersecurity specialist but as a strategic guardian of digital assets. The knowledge within these chapters serves as your toolkit, enabling you to navigate the ever-changing challenges of cyber threats confidently.

Prepare for an enlightening journey as we embark on this transformative guide. "Cybersecurity Guide" isn't just a handbook; it's your partner in the pursuit of cybersecurity mastery. Let's fortify your defenses and ensure that you stand resilient in the face of evolving digital challenges.

Chapter One

Understanding Cyber Threats

Exploring Common Cyber Threats Faced by Middles

In delving into the complex fabric of cybersecurity challenges faced by intermediate specialists, it becomes crucial to dissect the prevalent cyber threats that demand attention. As digital ecosystems expand and interconnect, the threat picture evolves, presenting numerous risks that necessitate a nuanced understanding.

One common threat faced by intermediates revolves around the deceptive maneuvers of phishing attacks. These covert actions often take the form of seemingly harmless emails or messages, seeking to entice unsuspecting users into divulging sensitive information. Consider the following React-based example, showcasing a potential phishing scenario:

```jsx
import React from 'react';

const DeceptiveEmail = () => {
  return (
    <div>
      <p>Hello [Recipient],</p>
```

```
        <p>We've noticed some unusual activity on your
account. Please click the following link to verify your
credentials:</p>
        <a href="http://malicious-site.com">Verify Now</a>
        <p>Thank you for your cooperation.</p>
    </div>
  );
};

export default DeceptiveEmail;
```

This seemingly harmless React component conceals the underlying threat, emphasizing the need for vigilance and user education to identify such phishing attempts.

Moving beyond the deceitful facade of phishing, intermediate specialists confront the persistent threat of malware. Malicious software infiltrates systems, often unnoticed, aiming to cause harm, steal data, or enable unauthorized access. Here, a simplified example illustrates a snippet of malicious code attempting to exploit a vulnerability:

```
import VulnerableComponent from 'vulnerable-package';

const exploitVulnerability = () => {
    // Malicious code attempting to exploit a vulnerability
in VulnerableComponent
    VulnerableComponent.exploit();
};
```

```
export default exploitVulnerability;
```

This scenario underscores the importance of robust vulnerability management and regular software updates to thwart potential exploits.

Furthermore, intermediate specialists must contend with the growing menace of ransomware attacks. In these instances, malicious actors encrypt critical data, demanding a ransom for its release. The following React snippet metaphorically captures the essence of a ransomware scenario:

```
import React, { useState } from 'react';

const RansomwareWarning = () => {
  const [encryptedData, setEncryptedData] = useState(true);

  return (
    <div>
      {encryptedData ? (
        <p>Your data has been encrypted. Pay the ransom to regain access.</p>
      ) : (
        <p>Data decryption successful. Access restored.</p>
      )}
    </div>
  );
};
```

```
export default RansomwareWarning;
```

This example serves as a symbolic representation of the disruptive impact of ransomware, highlighting the need for robust backup strategies and proactive security measures.

Lastly, the escalating concern of insider threats looms over intermediate specialists. Whether unintentional or malicious, insider threats emanate from within an organization, posing unique challenges. A React code snippet offers a conceptual illustration:

```
import React from 'react';

const InsiderThreatExample = () => {
  const employee = 'John Doe';
  const sensitiveData = 'Confidential Project Details';

  return (
    <div>
      <p>{employee} attempting to access {sensitiveData} without authorization.</p>
    </div>
  );
};

export default InsiderThreatExample;
```

This snippet encapsulates the nuanced nature of insider threats, emphasizing the necessity of robust access controls and continuous monitoring to mitigate potential risks.

In navigating the intricate tapestry of cyber threats, intermediate specialists must adopt a proactive stance. Recognizing the nuanced nature of these threats and implementing multifaceted defense strategies are crucial in fortifying digital defenses against the evolving cyber picture.

Case Studies on Recent Cyber Attacks

Delving into recent cyber attacks unveils concrete instances that highlight the dynamic nature of contemporary cybersecurity challenges. These real-world examples provide insights into the tactics employed by malicious actors, emphasizing the critical importance of vigilance and adaptive defense strategies.

One significant incident involved a sophisticated phishing campaign targeting a prominent financial institution. The attackers meticulously crafted emails that mimicked official communications, aiming to deceive recipients into clicking malicious links. A React-based representation of a phishing email, similar to those encountered in the campaign, can be envisioned as follows:

```jsx
import React from 'react';

const DeceptiveEmailExample = () => {
  return (
    <div>
      <p>Hello [Recipient],</p>
```

```
        <p>Your account security is at risk. Click the link
below to update your credentials:</p>
        <a href="http://malicious-link.com">Update Now</a>
        <p>Thank you for your prompt action.</p>
    </div>
  );
};

export default DeceptiveEmailExample;
```

This seemingly innocuous React component reflects the deceptive simplicity of phishing emails. Unsuspecting users within the targeted institution were lured into clicking malicious links, resulting in compromised credentials and unauthorized access.

In another incident, a multinational corporation fell victim to a targeted malware attack. Malicious actors exploited vulnerabilities in the company's software infrastructure, injecting a potent strain of malware. The following React snippet symbolizes the potential exploit of a vulnerability within a software component:

```
import VulnerableComponent from 'vulnerable-package';

const ExploitVulnerability = () => {
  // Malicious code attempting to exploit a vulnerability in VulnerableComponent
  VulnerableComponent.exploit();
};
```

```
export default ExploitVulnerability;
```

This case underscores the importance of robust vulnerability management practices and the urgent need for organizations to conduct regular software updates to mitigate potential risks.

Additionally, a ransomware attack on a healthcare institution demonstrated the dire consequences of data encryption. Malevolent actors infiltrated the institution's network, encrypting patient records and demanding a ransom for their release. A conceptual React snippet illustrates the essence of a ransomware scenario:

```
import React, { useState } from 'react';

const RansomwareExample = () => {
  const [encryptedData, setEncryptedData] = useState(true);

  return (
    <div>
      {encryptedData ? (
        <p>Your patient data has been encrypted. Pay the ransom to regain access.</p>
      ) : (
        <p>Data decryption successful. Access restored.</p>
      )}
    </div>
```

```
  );
};

export default RansomwareExample;
```

This symbolic representation emphasizes the disruptive impact of ransomware attacks on critical sectors, underscoring the urgency for robust backup strategies and proactive security measures.

In a notable insider threat case, a tech firm grappled with unauthorized data access by an employee. A React snippet serves as a conceptual illustration of an insider threat scenario:

```
import React from 'react';

const InsiderThreatExample = () => {
  const employee = 'John Doe';
  const sensitiveData = 'Confidential Project Details';

  return (
    <div>
      <p>{employee} attempting to access {sensitiveData} without authorization.</p>
    </div>
  );
};

export default InsiderThreatExample;
```

This example encapsulates the nuanced nature of insider threats, highlighting the necessity of robust access controls and continuous monitoring to mitigate potential risks originating from within the organization.

These case studies offer a glimpse into the harsh realities of the current cybersecurity landscape. They underscore the need for a proactive approach, constant vigilance, and a multifaceted defense strategy to thwart evolving cyber threats. By dissecting these real-world incidents, organizations can glean valuable insights to fortify their defenses and stay one step ahead of malicious actors.

Threat Intelligence and its Role in Defense

In the dynamic realm of cybersecurity, the strategic integration of Threat Intelligence emerges as a pivotal element in fortifying organizational defense mechanisms. Threat Intelligence, at its core, represents the distilled knowledge derived from the analysis of cyber threats and adversaries. It serves as a linchpin in proactive defense, enabling security teams to anticipate, respond, and mitigate potential risks.

One fundamental aspect of Threat Intelligence lies in its ability to contextualize cyber threats. By providing a detailed understanding of the tactics, techniques, and procedures (TTPs) employed by adversaries, Threat Intelligence equips security professionals with actionable insights. Consider the following React-based code snippet that metaphorically captures the essence of Threat Intelligence analysis:

```jsx
import React from 'react';

const ThreatIntelligenceAnalysis = () => {
  const analyzeThreat = (threatData) => {
    // Perform in-depth analysis of threat data
    // Extract TTPs and other relevant information
    // Provide actionable insights for defense
    return `Threat Intelligence Analysis: ${threatData}`;
  };

  return (
    <div>
      <p>Security Analyst conducting Threat Intelligence Analysis:</p>
      <code>{analyzeThreat("Malicious Activity X")}</code>
    </div>
  );
};

export default ThreatIntelligenceAnalysis;
```

This conceptual React component showcases the role of Threat Intelligence in analyzing and extracting actionable insights from specific threat data, aiding security analysts in making informed decisions.

Furthermore, Threat Intelligence serves as a compass for organizations navigating the turbulent waters of the cyber landscape. It enables security teams to prioritize threats based on relevance and potential impact, ensuring that resources are allocated efficiently. The React snippet below metaphorically illustrates the prioritization process:

```jsx
import React from 'react';

const ThreatPrioritization = () => {
  const prioritizeThreats = (threatList) => {
    // Prioritize threats based on relevance and potential impact
    // Allocate resources efficiently for defense
    return `Threats Prioritized: ${threatList}`;
  };

  return (
    <div>
      <p>Security Team Prioritizing Threats:</p>
      <code>{prioritizeThreats(["Threat A", "Threat B", "Threat C"])}</code>
    </div>
  );
};

export default ThreatPrioritization;
```

This React component conveys the role of Threat Intelligence in aiding security teams to systematically prioritize threats, allowing for a more focused and effective defense strategy.

Moreover, Threat Intelligence plays a crucial role in the development and enhancement of detection capabilities. By leveraging intelligence-driven insights, organizations can fine-tune their intrusion detection systems and security controls. The React snippet below symbolizes the integration of Threat Intelligence into the detection process:

```jsx
import React from 'react';

const ThreatDetectionEnhancement = () => {
  const enhanceDetection = (intelligenceInsights) => {
    // Integrate Threat Intelligence into detection systems
    // Fine-tune security controls based on intelligence-driven insights
    return `Detection Enhanced: ${intelligenceInsights}`;
  };

  return (
    <div>
      <p>Security Engineers Enhancing Threat Detection:</p>
      <code>{enhanceDetection("Insights from Threat Intelligence")}</code>
    </div>
  );
};

export default ThreatDetectionEnhancement;
```

This React component signifies the role of Threat Intelligence in enhancing detection capabilities, allowing security engineers to adapt and fortify their defenses against evolving threats.

In conclusion, Threat Intelligence stands as a cornerstone in the arsenal of cybersecurity defenses. Its role in contextualizing threats, prioritizing risks, and enhancing detection capabilities positions it as an invaluable asset for organizations seeking to navigate the intricate and ever-changing landscape of cybersecurity threats. The integration of Threat Intelligence into the defensive fabric empowers security professionals to not only respond to known threats but also to proactively anticipate and mitigate emerging risks.

Analyzing Attack Vectors and Entry Points

In the continually changing landscape of cybersecurity, a key element of proactive defense involves carefully examining attack vectors and entry points. Grasping how unauthorized entities infiltrate systems is crucial for security professionals aiming to strengthen their defenses and anticipate potential threats.

A common avenue for attacks is the exploitation of software vulnerabilities. Malicious actors frequently target flaws in software applications, seeking unauthorized access or compromising system integrity. Consider a simplified React code example to illustrate the concept of exploiting a vulnerability:

```
import VulnerableComponent from 'vulnerable-package';

const ExploitVulnerability = () => {
  // Malicious code attempting to exploit a vulnerability
in VulnerableComponent
  VulnerableComponent.exploit();
};

export default ExploitVulnerability;
```

This React component symbolizes the attempt to exploit a vulnerability in a software package, showcasing the potential entry point for attackers. Security teams must regularly assess vulnerabilities and apply timely patches to eliminate these weaknesses and mitigate potential risks.

Phishing attacks remain a widespread entry point for malicious actors. By tricking users into disclosing sensitive information, attackers can compromise security. A conceptual React snippet illustrates the deceptive nature of phishing:

```
import React from 'react';

const PhishingAttack = () => {
  return (
    <div>
      <p>Hello [Recipient],</p>
      <p>Your account security is at risk. Click the link below to update your credentials:</p>
      <a href="http://malicious-link.com">Update Now</a>
```

```
      <p>Thank you for your prompt action.</p>
    </div>
  );
};

export default PhishingAttack;
```

This React component signifies a phishing attack, where unsuspecting users may unintentionally provide credentials or sensitive information. Education and awareness programs are essential for users to recognize and thwart such phishing attempts.

Another noteworthy attack vector involves the exploitation of weak or compromised credentials. Attackers may gain unauthorized access through stolen or weak passwords. The following React code illustrates the potential unauthorized access scenario:

```
import React from 'react';

const CredentialExploitation = () => {
  const attemptUnauthorizedAccess = (username, password) => {
    // Malicious attempt to exploit weak or compromised credentials
    // Check if username and password match and grant unauthorized access
    return `Unauthorized Access Attempt: ${username}, ${password}`;
```

```
  };

  return (
    <div>
      <p>Malicious Actor attempting unauthorized access:</p>
      <code>{attemptUnauthorizedAccess("admin", "weakpassword")}</code>
    </div>
  );
};

export default CredentialExploitation;
```

This React component conceptually represents an unauthorized access attempt, emphasizing the importance of robust password policies, multi-factor authentication, and continuous monitoring to detect and mitigate such threats.

Moreover, supply chain attacks have become increasingly sophisticated entry points. Malicious actors target software dependencies or components in the supply chain, compromising the integrity of the final product. Although a complex scenario, a simplified React code snippet illustrates the concept:

```
import CompromisedDependency from 'compromised-package';

const SupplyChainAttack = () => {
  // Malicious code exploiting a compromised software dependency
  CompromisedDependency.exploit();
};

export default SupplyChainAttack;
```

This React component serves as a symbolic representation of a supply chain attack, underscoring the importance of rigorous vetting and monitoring of software dependencies to prevent potential compromise.

In conclusion, examining attack vectors and entry points is crucial for organizations aiming to fortify their cybersecurity defenses. By understanding potential avenues of compromise, security teams can implement proactive measures, conduct regular assessments, and fortify vulnerabilities to mitigate the ever-present risks in the dynamic field of cybersecurity. Furthermore, maintaining a vigilant stance against emerging threats and staying abreast of evolving cybersecurity trends becomes pivotal in proactively adapting defense strategies. This ongoing commitment ensures that organizations can effectively navigate the ever-changing landscape, fortifying their resilience against potential cybersecurity challenges.

Chapter Two

Building a Solid Foundation

Review of Fundamental Cybersecurity Principles

Delving into the essential pillars of cybersecurity, it is crucial to thoroughly assess the foundational principles that underpin the fortification of digital assets and systems. These principles act as guiding beacons in the cybersecurity cosmos, providing a necessary framework for organizations to establish robust defenses against a diverse array of potential threats.

A key principle involves the notion of least privilege, emphasizing the restriction of user access rights to the bare minimum required for their respective job functions. In a React-based context, envision a scenario where access privileges are meticulously managed:

```
import React from 'react';

const LeastPrivilegeExample = () => {
  const grantAccess = (user, privilegeLevel) => {
    // Function to grant access based on the principle of least privilege
    return `Access granted to ${user} with privilege level ${privilegeLevel}`;
  };

  return (
```

```
    <div>
        <p>Security System Enforcing Least Privilege:</p>
        <code>{grantAccess("UserA", "Read-Only")}</code>
    </div>
  );
};

export default LeastPrivilegeExample;
```

This React component signifies the adherence to the principle of least privilege, ensuring users are granted access only to the specific resources essential for their designated tasks, minimizing potential avenues for exploitation.

Another foundational principle revolves around the continuous monitoring of systems for potential security incidents. React code snippets can symbolically represent the vigilant eye of monitoring tools:

```
import React from 'react';

const ContinuousMonitoring = () => {
  const monitorSystem = () => {
    // Function to continuously monitor the system for security incidents
    return 'Continuous monitoring in progress';
  };

  return (
```

```
    <div>
        <p>Security Operations Center Engaged in Continuous
Monitoring:</p>
        <code>{monitorSystem()}</code>
    </div>
  );
};

export default ContinuousMonitoring;
```

This React component conceptually portrays the ongoing surveillance of systems, highlighting the significance of promptly identifying and responding to potential security incidents.

Incorporating a real-time visual representation, the React component underscores the vigilance required in overseeing systems for any signs of security vulnerabilities. It serves as a graphical reminder of the proactive stance needed to promptly address and mitigate potential threats in the dynamic landscape of digital security.

Encryption, a fundamental principle in cybersecurity, ensures that sensitive information remains confidential. A simplified React snippet illustrates the encryption process:

```jsx
import React from 'react';

const EncryptionExample = () => {
  const encryptData = (plaintext) => {
    // Function to encrypt sensitive data
    return `Encrypted Data: ${plaintext}`;
  };

  return (
    <div>
      <p>Cryptographic Module Performing Encryption:</p>
<code>{encryptData("SensitiveInformation123")}</code>
    </div>
  );
};

export default EncryptionExample;
```

This React component metaphorically portrays the application of encryption to safeguard sensitive information, underscoring its pivotal role in maintaining data confidentiality.

Moreover, the principle of defense-in-depth advocates for layered security mechanisms to mitigate potential risks comprehensively. Consider a React representation of this concept:

```jsx
import React from 'react';

const DefenseInDepthExample = () => {
  const implementLayers = () => {
    // Function to implement multiple layers of security
    return 'Defense-in-depth strategy implemented';
  };

  return (
    <div>
      <p>Security Architecture Adhering to Defense-in-Depth:</p>
      <code>{implementLayers()}</code>
    </div>
  );
};

export default DefenseInDepthExample;
```

This React component metaphorically captures the essence of defense-in-depth, illustrating the deployment of multiple security layers to fortify against various potential threats.

Lastly, the principle of patch management underscores the criticality of regularly updating software to address vulnerabilities. A React snippet symbolizes the importance of timely patching:

```jsx
import React from 'react';

const PatchManagementExample = () => {
  const applyPatch = () => {
    // Function to apply patches to software vulnerabilities
    return 'Patch applied successfully';
  };

  return (
    <div>
      <p>IT Team Performing Patch Management:</p>
      <code>{applyPatch()}</code>
    </div>
  );
};

export default PatchManagementExample;
```

This React component metaphorically represents the application of patches as a proactive measure to address vulnerabilities and enhance system security.

In essence, a holistic review of fundamental cybersecurity principles reveals their indispensable role in crafting resilient defense strategies. By adhering to these guiding principles, organizations can establish a robust cybersecurity posture, ensuring the protection of digital assets and fostering a secure digital environment.

Strengthening Network Security Basics

In the vast expanse of cybersecurity, reinforcing the foundational aspects of network security emerges as a crucial endeavor, vital for protecting sensitive data and upholding the integrity of digital infrastructures. This pursuit involves implementing essential measures that act as the primary defense against a diverse array of potential threats.

A key element of network security is the robust configuration of firewalls. These sentinels scrutinize incoming and outgoing network traffic, permitting or obstructing data packets based on predefined security rules. In a React-based portrayal, envision the establishment of firewall rules:

```
import React from 'react';

const FirewallConfiguration = () => {
  const configureFirewall = () => {
    // Function to set up firewall rules for network security
    return 'Firewall configured successfully';
  };

  return (
    <div>
      <p>Network Administrator Configuring Firewalls:</p>
      <code>{configureFirewall()}</code>
    </div>
  );
};
```

```
export default FirewallConfiguration;
```

This React component signifies the critical process of configuring firewalls to establish and enforce security policies, a fundamental step in thwarting unauthorized access.

Additionally, implementing secure wireless protocols is instrumental in preventing unauthorized access to networks. Utilizing advanced encryption protocols, such as WPA3, helps ensure the confidentiality of transmitted data. A simplified React snippet symbolizes the adoption of secure wireless protocols:

```
import React from 'react';

const WirelessSecurityExample = () => {
  const implementSecureWireless = () => {
    // Function to implement secure wireless protocols like WPA3
    return 'Secure wireless protocols implemented successfully';
  };

  return (
    <div>
      <p>Network Security Engineer Enhancing Wireless Security:</p>
      <code>{implementSecureWireless()}</code>
```

```
    </div>
  );
};

export default WirelessSecurityExample;
```

This React component metaphorically underscores the importance of adopting advanced wireless security protocols to mitigate the risk of unauthorized access and data interception.

Furthermore, the consistent monitoring of network traffic is imperative to identify and respond promptly to potential security incidents. In a React-based scenario, envision the vigilant oversight of network activities:

```
import React from 'react';

const NetworkTrafficMonitoring = () => {
  const monitorNetworkTraffic = () => {
    // Function to continuously monitor network traffic for security incidents
    return 'Continuous monitoring of network traffic in progress';
  };

  return (
    <div>
      <p>Security Analyst Monitoring Network Traffic:</p>
```

```
      <code>{monitorNetworkTraffic()}</code>
    </div>
  );
};

export default NetworkTrafficMonitoring;
```

This React component conceptually portrays the continuous surveillance of network traffic, emphasizing the significance of real-time monitoring to detect and respond to potential security threats.

As data flows seamlessly through this React component, its visual representation serves as a dynamic testament to the ongoing vigilance required in safeguarding against potential security threats. The emphasis on real-time monitoring underscores the proactive stance necessary for timely threat detection and swift response, ensuring the robust defense of network integrity.

Moreover, the judicious use of Virtual Private Networks (VPNs) enhances the security of data in transit by creating encrypted tunnels over public networks. A React-based representation symbolizes the establishment of a secure VPN connection:

```jsx
import React from 'react';

const VPNConfiguration = () => {
  const configureVPN = () => {
    // Function to configure Virtual Private Network
(VPN) for secure communication
    return 'VPN configured for secure communication';
  };

  return (
    <div>
      <p>IT Administrator Configuring VPN:</p>
      <code>{configureVPN()}</code>
    </div>
  );
};

export default VPNConfiguration;
```

This React component metaphorically signifies the importance of implementing VPNs to secure communication channels and protect data from potential eavesdropping.

Lastly, routine security audits and vulnerability assessments are crucial for identifying and rectifying potential weaknesses in network infrastructure. A React-based example envisions the execution of a security audit:

```jsx
import React from 'react';

const SecurityAuditExample = () => {
  const conductSecurityAudit = () => {
    // Function to conduct a security audit for network infrastructure
    return 'Security audit conducted successfully';
  };

  return (
    <div>
      <p>Cybersecurity Team Conducting Network Security Audit:</p>
      <code>{conductSecurityAudit()}</code>
    </div>
  );
};

export default SecurityAuditExample;
```

This React component metaphorically represents the proactive approach of cybersecurity teams in conducting security audits to identify and address vulnerabilities in network infrastructure.

In conclusion, fortifying the fundamentals of network security involves a meticulous approach to configuring firewalls, implementing secure wireless protocols, monitoring network traffic, utilizing VPNs, and conducting regular security audits.

These fundamental measures collectively contribute to establishing a robust network security posture, enhancing resilience against a dynamic landscape of potential threats.

Importance of Regular Security Audits

In the constantly changing landscape of digital security, the importance of regularly conducting security audits is undeniable. These audits play a crucial role in strengthening an organization's cybersecurity stance by taking a proactive approach to uncover vulnerabilities, assess potential risks, and maintain the ongoing integrity of sensitive data and systems.

One essential facet of these routine security audits involves a detailed examination of an organization's software and applications. Through thorough code analysis, security professionals can uncover potential weaknesses that could be exploited by malicious actors. Consider a React code scenario that emphasizes the significance of code reviews:

```
import React from 'react';

const CodeReviewExample = () => {
  const conductCodeReview = () => {
    // Function to perform a thorough code review for security vulnerabilities
    return 'Code review successfully completed, identifying potential vulnerabilities';
  };

  return (
    <div>
```

```
      <p>Security Analyst Carrying Out Code Review:</p>
      <code>{conductCodeReview()}</code>
    </div>
  );
};

export default CodeReviewExample;
```

This React component symbolizes the critical process of scrutinizing codebases for potential vulnerabilities, highlighting the proactive stance in identifying and rectifying security risks.

Additionally, regular security audits delve into the evaluation of access controls and user permissions. By assessing the adequacy of access levels, organizations can ensure that sensitive information is only accessible to authorized personnel. In a React-based depiction, consider a scenario where access control checks are emphasized:

```
import React from 'react';

const AccessControlAudit = () => {
  const assessAccessControls = () => {
    // Function to assess and audit access controls for user permissions
    return 'Access control audit successfully completed, ensuring proper user permissions';
```

```
  };

  return (
    <div>
      <p>Security Team Carrying Out Access Control Audit:</p>
      <code>{assessAccessControls()}</code>
    </div>
  );
};

export default AccessControlAudit;
```

This React component conceptually highlights the meticulous examination of access controls, underlining the importance of ensuring that only authorized users have appropriate levels of access.

Furthermore, the assessment of network configurations forms an integral part of security audits. By scrutinizing network settings, organizations can identify potential vulnerabilities or misconfigurations that might expose critical assets. In a React-based illustration, consider a snippet emphasizing network configuration assessments:

```jsx
import React from 'react';

const NetworkConfigurationAudit = () => {
  const auditNetworkConfigurations = () => {
    // Function to audit network configurations for
potential vulnerabilities or misconfigurations
    return 'Network configuration audit successfully completed, identifying potential risks';
  };

  return (
    <div>
      <p>IT Security Team Conducting Network Configuration Audit:</p>
      <code>{auditNetworkConfigurations()}</code>
    </div>
  );
};

export default NetworkConfigurationAudit;
```

This React component metaphorically represents the scrutiny of network configurations, underscoring the proactive approach in identifying and rectifying potential risks associated with network settings.

Regular security audits also contribute to incident response preparedness. By simulating real-world scenarios, organizations can evaluate their response mechanisms and fine-tune incident response plans. In a React-based representation, consider a snippet simulating an incident response exercise:

```
import React from 'react';

const IncidentResponseSimulation = () => {
  const simulateIncidentResponse = () => {
    // Function to simulate incident response scenarios and evaluate response effectiveness
    return 'Incident response simulation successfully completed, refining response strategies';
  };

  return (
    <div>
      <p>Cybersecurity Team Conducting Incident Response Simulation:</p>
      <code>{simulateIncidentResponse()}</code>
    </div>
  );
};

export default IncidentResponseSimulation;
```

This React component symbolizes the simulated assessment of incident response capabilities, emphasizing the continuous improvement of strategies to effectively counter potential security incidents.

In conclusion, the importance of regularly conducting security audits lies in their ability to proactively identify vulnerabilities, assess access controls, evaluate network configurations, and enhance incident response preparedness. By adopting a systematic approach to security audits, organizations can bolster their defenses, adapt to evolving threats, and cultivate a resilient cybersecurity posture that withstands the dynamic challenges in today's digital landscape.

Best Practices in Access Control and Identity Management

In the dynamic and ever-changing landscape of digital security, the implementation of robust practices for access control and identity management emerges as a crucial element in fortifying an organization's cybersecurity posture. These practices serve as a cornerstone in ensuring that only authorized individuals gain access to sensitive resources, thereby minimizing the risk of unauthorized data exposure and potential security breaches. By meticulously regulating access to critical resources, these practices not only bolster the organization's defense against cyber threats but also establish a proactive shield against unauthorized intrusions.

One exemplary practice in access control is the principle of least privilege, which advocates for granting users the minimal level of access required for them to fulfill their job responsibilities. In a React-based illustration, consider a snippet showcasing the application of the principle of least privilege:

```jsx
import React from 'react';

const LeastPrivilegeExample = () => {
  const grantAccess = (user, privilegeLevel) => {
    // Function to grant access based on the principle of least privilege
    return `Access granted to ${user} with privilege level ${privilegeLevel}`;
  };

  return (
    <div>
      <p>Security System Enforcing Least Privilege:</p>
      <code>{grantAccess("UserA", "Read-Only")}</code>
    </div>
  );
};

export default LeastPrivilegeExample;
```

This React component signifies the adherence to the principle of least privilege, ensuring users are granted access only to the specific resources essential for their designated tasks, thereby minimizing potential avenues for exploitation.

Moreover, the implementation of robust authentication mechanisms is paramount for secure access control. Multi-factor authentication (MFA) stands out as an effective practice, requiring users to provide multiple forms of identification before gaining access. In a React-based representation, envision a snippet emphasizing the use of MFA:

```jsx
import React from 'react';

const MultiFactorAuthentication = () => {
  const authenticateUser = (username, password, otp) => {
    // Function to authenticate user using multi-factor authentication
    return `User ${username} authenticated with password and OTP`;
  };

  return (
    <div>
      <p>Implementing Multi-Factor Authentication for Secure Access:</p>
      <code>{authenticateUser("UserA", "Password123", "123456")}</code>
    </div>
  );
};

export default MultiFactorAuthentication;
```

This React component metaphorically highlights the integration of multi-factor authentication, reinforcing the security of access control through an additional layer of user verification.

Additionally, the concept of role-based access control (RBAC) streamlines access management by assigning specific roles to users based on their responsibilities. In a React-based scenario, envision a snippet depicting the implementation of RBAC:

```
import React from 'react';

const RoleBasedAccessControl = () => {
  const assignRole = (user, role) => {
    // Function to assign a role to a user in role-based access control
    return `Role ${role} assigned to user ${user}`;
  };

  return (
    <div>
      <p>Implementing Role-Based Access Control for Streamlined Access Management:</p>
      <code>{assignRole("UserA", "Admin")}</code>
    </div>
  );
};

export default RoleBasedAccessControl;
```

This React component conceptually portrays the application of role-based access control, ensuring that users are granted access based on their designated roles within the organization.

Moreover, continuous monitoring of user activities is pivotal for detecting and responding to potential security incidents promptly. In a React-based illustration, consider a snippet highlighting the importance of user activity monitoring:

```
import React from 'react';

const UserActivityMonitoring = () => {
  const monitorUserActivity = () => {
    // Function to continuously monitor user activities for security incidents
    return 'Continuous monitoring of user activities in progress';
  };

  return (
    <div>
      <p>Security Analyst Monitoring User Activities:</p>
      <code>{monitorUserActivity()}</code>
    </div>
  );
};

export default UserActivityMonitoring;
```

This React component metaphorically represents the continuous surveillance of user activities, underscoring the significance of real-time monitoring to detect and respond to potential security threats.

In conclusion, adopting best practices in access control and identity management, such as the principle of least privilege, multi-factor authentication, role-based access control, and continuous user activity monitoring, is paramount for organizations aiming to establish a resilient cybersecurity defense. These practices collectively contribute to minimizing the risk of unauthorized access, safeguarding sensitive data, and fortifying the overall security posture of the organization in the dynamic landscape of digital security.

As the React component visually captures the continuous surveillance of user activities, it serves as a tangible reminder of the proactive measures necessary to ensure a vigilant cybersecurity posture. The implementation of best practices in access control and identity management not only safeguards against potential threats but also fosters a culture of resilience, aligning organizations with the dynamic demands of digital security.

Chapter Three

Advanced Endpoint Protection

Evolution of Endpoint Security Solutions

In the dynamic landscape of securing digital environments, the trajectory of endpoint security solutions has undergone a noteworthy evolution, propelled by the continuous quest for resilience against an ever-changing threat scenario. This evolution is not simply a chronological progression but a strategic adjustment to the complexities of contemporary cybersecurity challenges.

Beginning in the early era of computing, conventional antivirus solutions emerged as the pioneers in endpoint security. These solutions relied on signature-based detection mechanisms, scanning files for known patterns of malicious code. In a React-based depiction, imagine a simplified representation of signature-based detection:

```
import React from 'react';

const AntivirusSignatureDetection = () => {
  const scanFile = (file) => {
    // Function to scan a file for known signatures using traditional antivirus
    return `File examined for known signatures: ${file}`;
  };

  return (
```

```
    <div>
      <p>Traditional Antivirus Utilizing Signature Detection:</p>
      <code>{scanFile("malicious_file.exe")}</code>
    </div>
  );
};

export default AntivirusSignatureDetection;
```

This React component symbolizes the initial stage of endpoint security, where antivirus solutions depended on recognizing predefined patterns of malicious code.

As cyber threats evolved, so did the necessity for more sophisticated protection mechanisms. Heuristic-based detection emerged as a subsequent step, aiming to identify previously unseen threats by analyzing behavior patterns. In a React-based illustration, consider a snippet showcasing heuristic-based detection:

```
import React from 'react';

const HeuristicDetection = () => {
  const analyzeBehavior = (file) => {
    // Function to analyze the behavior of a file using heuristic-based detection
    return `Behavioral analysis conducted on file: ${file}`;
```

```
  };

  return (
    <div>
      <p>Endpoint Security Employing Heuristic
Detection:</p>
      <code>{analyzeBehavior("new_malware.exe")}</code>
    </div>
  );
};

export default HeuristicDetection;
```

This React component represents the evolution towards heuristic-based detection, where endpoint security solutions started to assess the behavior of files to detect potential threats proactively.

In response to the escalating sophistication of cyber threats, machine learning and artificial intelligence (AI) have become integral components of modern endpoint security solutions. These technologies enable systems to continuously learn and adapt, enhancing the accuracy of threat detection. In a React-based portrayal, envision a snippet showcasing the integration of machine learning:

```jsx
import React from 'react';

const MachineLearningIntegration = () => {
  const applyMachineLearning = (file) => {
    // Function to apply machine learning for dynamic threat detection
    return `Machine learning algorithms applied to analyze file: ${file}`;
  };

  return (
    <div>
      <p>Advanced Endpoint Security with Machine Learning Integration:</p>
      <code>{applyMachineLearning("sophisticated_malware.exe")}</code>
    </div>
  );
};

export default MachineLearningIntegration;
```

This React component emphasizes the utilization of machine learning algorithms to enhance the adaptability of endpoint security solutions against dynamic and evolving threats.

Moreover, the advent of endpoint detection and response (EDR) solutions marked a paradigm shift. EDR goes beyond traditional prevention methods, focusing on swift detection and response to security incidents. In a React-based illustration, consider a snippet depicting the functionality of an EDR solution:

```jsx
import React from 'react';

const EndpointDetectionResponse = () => {
  const detectAndRespond = (incident) => {
    // Function to detect and respond to security incidents using EDR solutions
    return `Security incident detected and responded to: ${incident}`;
  };

  return (
    <div>
      <p>Endpoint Detection and Response (EDR) in Action:</p>
      <code>{detectAndRespond("suspicious_activity_detected")}</code>
    </div>
  );
};

export default EndpointDetectionResponse;
```

This React component conceptually signifies the proactive approach of EDR solutions, focusing on rapid incident detection and response to mitigate potential security risks effectively.

In conclusion, the evolution of endpoint security solutions has traversed a continuum, from traditional antivirus measures to heuristic-based detection, machine learning integration, and the advent of EDR solutions. This journey underscores the relentless pursuit of staying ahead of cyber adversaries, adapting strategies and technologies to fortify the resilience of endpoint security in the face of an ever-changing threat landscape.

Implementing Robust Endpoint Detection and Response (EDR)

In the constantly shifting dynamics of digital security, the implementation of a robust Endpoint Detection and Response (EDR) strategy has become essential for organizations aiming to strengthen their defenses against sophisticated cyber threats. EDR goes beyond traditional security measures, offering a proactive approach that focuses on swift detection, response, and mitigation of security incidents, ensuring a resilient cybersecurity posture.

The foundation of a robust EDR system lies in its ability to continuously monitor and analyze endpoint activities. This involves scrutinizing system logs, network traffic, and file behaviors in real-time. In a React-based representation, envision a simplified snippet depicting the real-time monitoring aspect:

```
import React from 'react';

const RealTimeMonitoring = () => {
  const monitorEndpointActivities = () => {
    // Function to continuously monitor endpoint activities in real-time
    return 'Ongoing real-time monitoring of endpoint activities';
  };

  return (
    <div>
      <p>EDR System Engaged in Real-Time Monitoring:</p>
      <code>{monitorEndpointActivities()}</code>
    </div>
  );
};

export default RealTimeMonitoring;
```

This React component signifies the continuous surveillance of endpoint activities, highlighting the proactive stance of an EDR system.

Detection mechanisms in EDR systems often leverage behavioral analysis to identify anomalies that could signify potential security threats. By establishing a baseline of normal behavior, the system can flag deviations that may indicate malicious activity. In a React-based illustration, consider a simplified snippet representing behavioral analysis:

```jsx
import React from 'react';

const BehavioralAnalysis = () => {
  const analyzeBehavior = (endpoint) => {
    // Function to perform behavioral analysis on endpoint activities
    return `Behavioral analysis performed on endpoint: ${endpoint}`;
  };

  return (
    <div>
      <p>Implementing Behavioral Analysis in EDR:</p>
      <code>{analyzeBehavior("Endpoint123")}</code>
    </div>
  );
};

export default BehavioralAnalysis;
```

This React component metaphorically emphasizes the utilization of behavioral analysis to detect deviations from normal endpoint behavior, enhancing the precision of threat identification.

In addition to behavioral analysis, signature-based detection remains a valuable component of EDR systems. By comparing file characteristics and behaviors against known patterns of malicious code, EDR can swiftly identify and mitigate familiar threats. In a React-based portrayal, consider a snippet showcasing signature-based detection:

```jsx
import React from 'react';

const SignatureBasedDetection = () => {
  const detectMaliciousFile = (file) => {
    // Function to detect a malicious file using signature-based detection in EDR
    return `Detected malicious file: ${file}`;
  };

  return (
    <div>
      <p>Utilizing Signature-Based Detection in EDR:</p>
      <code>{detectMaliciousFile("malware_file.exe")}</code>
    </div>
  );
};

export default SignatureBasedDetection;
```

This React component signifies the integration of signature-based detection in EDR, acknowledging its effectiveness in swiftly identifying known threats.

Once a potential threat is identified, the response component of EDR becomes crucial. EDR systems enable automated responses and proactive mitigation measures. In a React-based conceptualization, envision a snippet depicting the response phase:

```
import React from 'react';

const AutomatedResponse = () => {
  const initiateResponse = (threat) => {
    // Function to initiate automated response and mitigation in EDR
    return `Initiated automated response for identified threat: ${threat}`;
  };

  return (
    <div>
      <p>Automated Response and Mitigation in EDR:</p>
      <code>{initiateResponse("PotentialThreat123")}</code>
    </div>
  );
};

export default AutomatedResponse;
```

This React component metaphorically represents the automated response initiated by an EDR system upon identifying a potential threat, showcasing the efficiency of proactive mitigation measures.

Furthermore, EDR systems facilitate detailed forensic analysis post-incident. This involves examining the timeline of events, identifying the root cause, and refining future prevention strategies. In a React-based scenario, consider a snippet illustrating post-incident forensic analysis:

```
import React from 'react';

const ForensicAnalysis = () => {
  const conductForensicAnalysis = (incident) => {
    // Function to conduct forensic analysis on a security incident in EDR
    return `Conducted forensic analysis on security incident: ${incident}`;
  };

  return (
    <div>
      <p>Post-Incident Forensic Analysis in EDR:</p>
      <code>{conductForensicAnalysis("SecurityIncident456")}</code>
    </div>
  );
};
```

```
export default ForensicAnalysis;
```

This React component conceptually signifies the meticulous forensic analysis conducted by EDR systems, contributing to an in-depth understanding of security incidents.

In conclusion, the implementation of robust Endpoint Detection and Response (EDR) is paramount in the contemporary cybersecurity landscape. With its focus on real-time monitoring, behavioral analysis, signature-based detection, automated response, and post-incident forensic analysis, EDR emerges as a proactive and effective strategy for organizations seeking to fortify their cybersecurity defenses against the ever-changing threat landscape.

Behavioral Analysis for Threat Detection

In the intricate world of cybersecurity, the crucial role played by Behavioral Analysis in Threat Detection stands out significantly. This method goes beyond traditional approaches, offering a dynamic and proactive means of identifying potential security threats. Behavioral Analysis involves a meticulous examination of digital behaviors, aiming to discern anomalies that may indicate malicious activity within a digital environment.

Consider a simplified React-based representation that encapsulates the essence of Behavioral Analysis for Threat Detection:

```jsx
import React from 'react';

const BehavioralAnalysisComponent = () => {
  const analyzeBehavior = (endpoint) => {
    // Function to perform behavioral analysis on endpoint activities
    return `Conducted behavioral analysis on endpoint: ${endpoint}`;
  };

  return (
    <div>
      <p>Behavioral Analysis for Threat Detection in Action:</p>
      <code>{analyzeBehavior("Endpoint123")}</code>
    </div>
  );
};

export default BehavioralAnalysisComponent;
```

This React component metaphorically illustrates the application of Behavioral Analysis, emphasizing its capability to scrutinize endpoint behaviors for potential signs of malicious intent.

The core of Behavioral Analysis lies in establishing a baseline of normal behavior for digital entities, such as endpoints or users. By understanding what is considered typical, the system can more effectively flag deviations that may indicate suspicious or anomalous activities. This React-based snippet conceptualizes the establishment of a baseline:

```jsx
import React from 'react';

const EstablishBaselineComponent = () => {
  const establishBaseline = (entity) => {
    // Function to establish a baseline of normal behavior for an entity
    return `Establishing baseline for ${entity}`;
  };

  return (
    <div>
      <p>Establishing Baseline for Behavioral Analysis:</p>
      <code>{establishBaseline("User123")}</code>
    </div>
  );
};

export default EstablishBaselineComponent;
```

This React component signifies the crucial step of establishing a baseline for entities, enabling the system to discern patterns of normal behavior against which potential anomalies can be identified.

Behavioral Analysis often involves scrutinizing various parameters such as system logins, access patterns, and data retrieval activities. In a React-based scenario, envision a snippet that encapsulates the analysis of diverse behavioral parameters:

```jsx
import React from 'react';

const DiverseBehavioralAnalysisComponent = () => {
  const analyzeDiverseBehaviors = (user) => {
    // Function to analyze diverse behaviors of a user for threat detection
    return `Analyzing diverse behaviors of user: ${user}`;
  };

  return (
    <div>
      <p>Diverse Behavioral Analysis for Threat Detection:</p>
      <code>{analyzeDiverseBehaviors("User456")}</code>
    </div>
  );
};

export default DiverseBehavioralAnalysisComponent;
```

This React component symbolizes the multifaceted nature of Behavioral Analysis, showcasing its ability to delve into diverse behaviors exhibited by users or entities to pinpoint potential security threats.

Behavioral Analysis becomes particularly powerful when coupled with machine learning algorithms. In this React-based snippet, envision the integration of machine learning for enhanced precision in identifying deviations:

```
import React from 'react';

const MachineLearningIntegrationComponent = () => {
  const applyMachineLearning = (behavior) => {
    // Function to apply machine learning for enhanced precision in threat detection
    return `Applying machine learning to analyze behavior: ${behavior}`;
  };

  return (
    <div>
      <p>Enhancing Behavioral Analysis with Machine Learning:</p>
      <code>{applyMachineLearning("SuspiciousBehavior123")}</code>
    </div>
  );
};

export default MachineLearningIntegrationComponent;
```

This React component metaphorically emphasizes the amalgamation of Behavioral Analysis with machine learning, showcasing its potential to enhance the accuracy and adaptability of threat detection mechanisms.

In conclusion, Behavioral Analysis for Threat Detection emerges as a proactive and sophisticated approach within the cybersecurity landscape. By scrutinizing behaviors, establishing baselines, analyzing diverse parameters, and integrating machine learning, this method provides organizations with a powerful tool to identify potential security threats before they manifest into larger issues. The adoption of Behavioral Analysis represents a strategic move towards a more proactive and adaptive cybersecurity posture in the face of evolving digital risks.

Balancing Security and User Experience

In the intricate interplay of modern cybersecurity, there arises a pivotal challenge—finding the delicate balance between implementing robust security measures and ensuring a seamless user experience.

Organizations, as they endeavor to fortify their digital defenses, grapple with the imperative of safeguarding their users without unintentionally impeding the usability and satisfaction they derive from digital interactions.

This multifaceted challenge underscores the need for organizations to continuously adapt their cybersecurity strategies, ensuring a dynamic synergy between user-centricity and effective threat mitigation.

Consider a practical scenario where a React-based authentication system exemplifies the concept of harmonizing security and user experience:

```jsx
import React, { useState } from 'react';

const AuthenticationComponent = () => {
  const [username, setUsername] = useState('');
  const [password, setPassword] = useState('');
  const [authenticated, setAuthenticated] = useState(false);

  const authenticateUser = () => {
    // Simulating authentication logic
    if (username === 'secureUser' && password === 'strongPassword') {
      setAuthenticated(true);
    } else {
      setAuthenticated(false);
    }
  };

  return (
    <div>
      {!authenticated ? (
        <div>
          <label>Username:</label>
          <input type="text" value={username} onChange={(e) => setUsername(e.target.value)} />
          <br />
```

```
        <label>Password:</label>
        <input type="password" value={password}
onChange={(e) => setPassword(e.target.value)} />
        <br />
        <button
onClick={authenticateUser}>Login</button>
      </div>
     ) : (
        <p>User successfully authenticated! Welcome to a
secure and user-friendly environment.</p>
      )}
    </div>
  );
};

export default AuthenticationComponent;
```

This React component embodies a straightforward authentication mechanism where users input their credentials. The code reflects the challenge of creating an interface that seamlessly integrates security measures while ensuring user-friendly interaction.

Achieving the right equilibrium demands a nuanced approach. Rigorous security measures, such as intricate password requirements and multifactor authentication, contribute to a safer digital space. However, an excessive focus on these measures might lead to a cumbersome user experience, potentially causing frustration and discouraging users from actively participating in the platform.

For example, envision a scenario where password complexity requirements are integrated into a React-based registration form:

```
import React, { useState } from 'react';

const RegistrationForm = () => {
  const [password, setPassword] = useState('');
  const [passwordError, setPasswordError] = useState('');

  const validatePassword = () => {
    // Simulating password complexity validation
    if (password.length < 8) {
      setPasswordError('Password must be at least 8 characters long');
    } else {
      setPasswordError('');
    }
  };

  return (
    <div>
      <label>Create Password:</label>
      <input
        type="password"
        value={password}
        onChange={(e) => setPassword(e.target.value)}
```

```
      onBlur={validatePassword}
    />
    {passwordError && <p>{passwordError}</p>}
  </div>
  );
};

export default RegistrationForm;
```

This React component illustrates how password complexity requirements can be enforced. While such measures enhance security, they can potentially create friction for users who may find it cumbersome to meet intricate criteria.

Strategies to strike a balance involve implementing security measures discreetly in the background without compromising the user experience. For instance, seamless biometric authentication methods or adaptive authentication that assesses risk in real-time contribute to a more user-friendly interaction while maintaining robust security standards.

Incorporating adaptive security measures into the user interface involves leveraging React or similar frameworks to dynamically adjust security protocols based on user behavior, device characteristics, and contextual factors. However, the underlying security mechanisms remain formidable, ensuring a secure digital environment.

Harmonizing security and user experience is an ongoing process that demands continuous refinement. Organizations must stay attuned to user feedback, evolving threat landscapes, and advancements in technology to strike an optimal balance that fosters a secure and satisfying digital experience for users. The key lies in seamlessly integrating stringent security measures with an intuitive and frictionless user interface, creating a digital ecosystem where both security and user experience coexist seamlessly.

Chapter Four

Easy-to-Follow Advanced Cybersecurity Tactics

Importance of Secure Software Development

In the dynamic context of contemporary software development, the emphasis on implementing robust security measures at every stage has risen to a position of utmost importance. Integrating these security practices is crucial, as the repercussions of overlooking security can be severe, ranging from data breaches to compromised user privacy.

Imagine a scenario where a React-based web application exemplifies secure software development practices:

```
import React, { useState } from 'react';

const SecureLoginForm = () => {
  const [username, setUsername] = useState('');
  const [password, setPassword] = useState('');
  const [authenticated, setAuthenticated] = useState(false);

  const authenticateUser = () => {
    // Simulating secure authentication logic with proper input validation
    const sanitizedUsername = sanitizeInput(username);
    const sanitizedPassword = sanitizeInput(password);
```

```jsx
    if (sanitizedUsername === 'secureUser' && sanitizedPassword === 'strongPassword') {
      setAuthenticated(true);
    } else {
      setAuthenticated(false);
    }
  };

  const sanitizeInput = (input) => {
    // Function to sanitize input and prevent common security vulnerabilities
    return input.trim();
  };

  return (
    <div>
      {!authenticated ? (
        <div>
          <label>Username:</label>
          <input type="text" value={username} onChange={(e) => setUsername(e.target.value)} />
          <br />
          <label>Password:</label>
          <input type="password" value={password} onChange={(e) => setPassword(e.target.value)} />
          <br />
          <button onClick={authenticateUser}>Login</button>
```

```
        </div>
      ) : (
        <p>User successfully authenticated! Welcome to a secure environment.</p>
      )}
    </div>
  );
};

export default SecureLoginForm;
```

This React component showcases a secure login form that integrates input validation to mitigate common security vulnerabilities. Sanitizing user inputs is a fundamental practice in preventing attacks such as SQL injection and cross-site scripting.

Secure software development commences with a proactive mindset, addressing potential vulnerabilities from the outset. The adoption of secure coding practices, including input validation, output encoding, and parameterized queries, significantly reduces the risk of exploitation by malicious actors.

For example, envision a React component that highlights the importance of output encoding to prevent cross-site scripting (XSS) attacks:

```jsx
import React from 'react';

const SecureOutputComponent = () => {
  const maliciousInput = '<script>alert("XSS attack!")</script>';
  const sanitizedOutput = encodeOutput(maliciousInput);

  const encodeOutput = (input) => {
    // Function to encode output to prevent XSS attacks
    return input.replace(/</g, '&lt;').replace(/>/g, '&gt;');
  };

  return (
    <div>
      <p>Original Input: {maliciousInput}</p>
      <p>Sanitized Output: {sanitizedOutput}</p>
    </div>
  );
};

export default SecureOutputComponent;
```

This React component illustrates the significance of encoding output to thwart potential XSS attacks. By replacing special characters with their HTML entities, developers can ensure that user-generated content is rendered safely.

In the context of secure software development, staying informed about the latest security vulnerabilities and adhering to established security standards is indispensable. Regular code reviews, security audits, and continuous integration of security testing tools contribute to a robust defense against potential exploits.

Furthermore, incorporating secure authentication mechanisms, such as multi-factor authentication, strengthens the overall security posture of applications. While the React component below is a simplified representation, it conveys the essence of integrating multi-factor authentication for enhanced security:

```
import React, { useState } from 'react';

const MultiFactorAuthComponent = () => {
  const [username, setUsername] = useState('');
  const [password, setPassword] = useState('');
  const [authenticated, setAuthenticated] = useState(false);

  const authenticateUser = () => {
    // Simulating secure authentication logic with multi-factor authentication
    const sanitizedUsername = sanitizeInput(username);
    const sanitizedPassword = sanitizeInput(password);

    if (
      sanitizedUsername === 'secureUser' &&
      sanitizedPassword === 'strongPassword' &&
```

```
      validateMultiFactorAuth()
  ) {
    setAuthenticated(true);
  } else {
    setAuthenticated(false);
  }
};

const validateMultiFactorAuth = () => {
  // Simulating multi-factor authentication validation
  return true; // In a real-world scenario, this would involve additional verification steps
};

// ... (Rest of the component)

return (
  // ... (JSX for the component)
);
};

export default MultiFactorAuthComponent;
```

This React component illustrates a secure authentication process that incorporates multi-factor authentication, an additional layer of protection against unauthorized access.

In conclusion, the significance of secure software development cannot be overstated in today's digital landscape. It goes beyond the mere implementation of security features; it involves cultivating a security-centric mindset among developers, adopting best practices, and remaining vigilant against emerging threats. By integrating secure coding principles at the core of the development process, organizations can mitigate risks, protect sensitive data, and build a foundation for robust and resilient software applications.

Common Vulnerabilities and Exploits

In the constantly changing digital sphere, the persistence of Common Vulnerabilities and Exploits (CVEs) remains a consistent challenge for cybersecurity professionals. These vulnerabilities, often rooted in coding oversights or misconfigurations, open doors for malicious actors to exploit systems and compromise sensitive data. This article delves into the details of common vulnerabilities, shedding light on the technical nuances that underlie these exploitable weaknesses.

One widespread vulnerability type is Injection Attacks, where untrusted data is improperly processed within a program's code. SQL Injection, for example, poses an enduring concern. Picture a scenario where a web application interacts with a database to retrieve user information:

```
const userInput = req.query.username;
const query = "SELECT * FROM Users WHERE username = '" + userInput + "';";
```

In this snippet, if an attacker provides malicious input like **'; DROP TABLE Users; --**, the resulting query becomes:

```
SELECT * FROM Users WHERE username = ''; DROP TABLE Users; --';
```

This straightforward yet powerful injection can lead to catastrophic consequences, causing data loss or unauthorized access.

Cross-Site Scripting (XSS) is another vulnerability that allows attackers to inject malicious scripts into web pages viewed by other users. Imagine a React component rendering user-generated content:

```
function Comment({ text }) {
  return <div dangerouslySetInnerHTML={{ __html: text }} />;
}
```

If this component is used without proper input validation, an attacker could insert a script like:

```
<script>alert('XSS Attack');</script>
```

When this comment is rendered, the script executes, posing a security risk to users.

Authentication and session management vulnerabilities are critical, impacting user access and data protection directly. Weak passwords, insufficiently hashed credentials, and insecure session handling can lead to unauthorized access. Consider a React authentication flow:

```
// Simplified authentication function
function authenticateUser(username, password) {
  // Check if username and password match stored credentials
  if (username === storedUsername && password === storedPassword) {
    // Generate session token
    const token = generateToken();
    return token;
  } else {
    // Authentication failed
    return null;
  }
}
```

Inadequate validation or secure token generation can expose vulnerabilities, enabling attackers to compromise user accounts.

Security misconfigurations represent a common pitfall, arising from oversight in system configurations. Improperly configured servers, databases, or cloud services can provide an entry point for unauthorized access. For instance, an improperly configured React app may inadvertently expose sensitive information:

```
// Insecurely storing API key
const apiKey = process.env.REACT_APP_API_KEY;
```

If the React app is configured to expose environment variables in the client-side code, an attacker can easily access the API key, potentially leading to unauthorized API access.

To mitigate these vulnerabilities, a proactive approach is imperative. Regular code audits, vulnerability assessments, and penetration testing play pivotal roles in identifying and addressing potential weaknesses. The development and adoption of secure coding practices, such as input validation, proper authentication mechanisms, and secure configuration, serve as robust deterrents against exploitation.

Security patches and updates must be promptly applied to address known vulnerabilities in third-party libraries and dependencies. Additionally, incorporating security measures into the software development life cycle, from design to deployment, fosters a security-first mindset.

In conclusion, the battle against Common Vulnerabilities and Exploits is an ongoing endeavor, demanding vigilance, expertise, and a commitment to secure coding practices. The technical details involved necessitate a comprehensive understanding of potential weaknesses and the implementation of robust security measures. As the digital landscape continues to change, the pursuit of a secure and resilient cybersecurity environment remains a paramount objective for the cybersecurity community.

Code Review Best Practices

In the domain of software development, the importance of thorough code review processes cannot be overstressed. Code review serves as a pivotal element in ensuring the quality, maintainability, and security of software. Adopting best practices in this critical phase of the development cycle is essential for fostering a collaborative and efficient environment. This discussion delves into essential code review practices, shedding light on practical approaches that contribute to the overall excellence of software engineering.

Initially, an important aspect of effective code reviews lies in maintaining a clear and well-defined scope. Focusing on specific aspects such as functionality, readability, and adherence to coding standards ensures a comprehensive yet targeted assessment. For instance, in a React application, consider the following code snippet:

```
// Inefficient component rendering
function InefficientComponent({ data }) {
  const result = processData(data);
  return <div>{result}</div>;
}
```

In this example, a code reviewer might address concerns about efficiency, suggesting optimizations for the **processData** function to enhance performance.

Furthermore, fostering a constructive and collaborative atmosphere is crucial during code reviews. Instead of using a critical tone, reviewers should provide feedback with a focus on improvement. For instance:

```
// Unclear variable names
function ExampleComponent({ x, y }) {
  const result = calculateSum(x, y);
  return <div>{result}</div>;
}
```

Constructive feedback could involve recommending more descriptive variable names, enhancing code readability without sacrificing functionality.

Maintaining a consistent coding style is crucial for maintainability and collaboration. Enforcing a standardized style guide, such as Airbnb's React Style Guide, aids in creating a cohesive codebase. For instance:

```
// Inconsistent indentation
function InconsistentComponent() {
  const value = getValue();
return (
  <div>
      {value}
    </div>
);
}
```

Reviewers may highlight inconsistent indentation and suggest aligning the code according to the established style guide for better code uniformity.

Incorporating automated tools into the code review process enhances efficiency and accuracy. Tools like ESLint for static code analysis can automatically catch common issues and enforce coding standards. For instance:

```
// ESLint warning
function ESLintExample() {
  const value = getValue();
  return <div>{value}</div>;
}
```

An ESLint warning might prompt the developer to address potential issues, fostering a proactive approach to code quality.

Additionally, code reviews should prioritize the identification of potential security vulnerabilities. Reviewers should be vigilant in assessing code for common security pitfalls. For instance:

```
// Insecure data handling
function InsecureComponent({ userData }) {
  const formattedData = processData(userData);
  return <div>{formattedData}</div>;
}
```

A code reviewer might flag concerns about insecure data handling and advocate for validating and sanitizing user input to mitigate security risks.

Concerning version control systems, ensuring that code reviews are conducted on feature branches before merging into the main branch helps maintain a stable and reliable codebase. It prevents introducing incomplete or unstable code into the main code repository. For instance:

```
// Feature branch code
function FeatureBranchComponent() {
  // New feature implementation
  return <div>New feature</div>;
}
```

Conducting code reviews on the feature branch allows for a thorough evaluation of the new feature's implementation before it is integrated into the main codebase.

In conclusion, code review best practices serve as the foundation of software development excellence. By adhering to clear scope definitions, fostering a positive feedback culture, enforcing coding standards, leveraging automated tools, prioritizing security considerations, and conducting reviews on feature branches, development teams can elevate the quality and reliability of their codebase. Embracing these practices ensures that the collaborative effort of software engineering culminates in the delivery of high-quality, secure, and maintainable software products.

Integrating Security into the Software Development Lifecycle (SDLC)

In the dynamic scope of software development, it becomes crucial to seamlessly weave security measures into the Software Development Lifecycle (SDLC). This strategic methodology ensures that security considerations are not relegated to an afterthought but are seamlessly integrated into every phase of the development process. This exploration of the interplay between security and SDLC reveals practical methodologies that fortify the integrity of software applications.

One foundational principle involves initiating security measures at the inception of a project, during the requirements gathering phase. This entails a meticulous examination of potential security risks and the establishment of security requirements. For instance, in a React application, the definition of secure user authentication requirements could be explicit:

```
// Security requirement for user authentication
const secureAuthenticationRequirements = {
  // Enforce strong password policies
  passwordPolicy: {
    minLength: 8,
    requireUpperCase: true,
    requireLowerCase: true,
    requireNumbers: true,
    requireSpecialCharacters: true,
  },
```

```
// Implement account lockout after multiple failed
login attempts
  accountLockout: {
    maxAttempts: 3,
    lockoutDuration: 15 * 60 * 1000, // 15 minutes
  },
};
```

By incorporating such security requirements into the initial project specifications, development teams set the stage for a proactive security posture.

Moving into the design phase, secure architecture and coding practices become pivotal considerations. This involves selecting frameworks and libraries with a demonstrated commitment to security, such as React's emphasis on component-based architecture. Moreover, developers should adhere to secure coding practices to mitigate vulnerabilities. For example, in React development:

```
// Secure coding practice: Input validation to prevent
XSS attacks
function Comment({ text }) {
  const sanitizedText = sanitizeInput(text);
  return <div>{sanitizedText}</div>;
}

function sanitizeInput(input) {
  // Implement input validation to prevent XSS attacks
```

```
// (Implementation details omitted for brevity)
// ...
}
```

Here, the **sanitizeInput** function represents a secure coding practice, implementing input validation to prevent Cross-Site Scripting (XSS) attacks.

As the development phase progresses, incorporating security testing becomes integral. Automated tools, like static code analyzers and security scanners, can play a crucial role in identifying potential vulnerabilities. For instance, leveraging tools such as ESLint for static code analysis in React applications aids in the automatic detection of security issues:

```
// ESLint security warning
function InsecureComponent() {
  // Code with a security vulnerability
  const userInput = getUserInput();
  return <div>{userInput}</div>;
}
```

ESLint, configured with security rules, can generate warnings for insecure code patterns, prompting developers to rectify potential vulnerabilities promptly.

The implementation of secure deployment practices is equally vital. Employing secure configuration settings, encrypting sensitive data, and ensuring secure communication channels help mitigate risks during deployment. In a React deployment scenario, securing environment variables is critical:

```
// Secure deployment practice: Protecting sensitive
information
const apiKey = process.env.REACT_APP_API_KEY;
```

Here, adopting secure practices involves protecting sensitive information, such as API keys, by ensuring they are stored and accessed securely within the deployment environment.

Post-deployment, ongoing monitoring and maintenance are indispensable components of a holistic security strategy. Regularly updating dependencies, monitoring for emerging threats, and swiftly addressing security incidents contribute to the longevity of a secure application. For example:

```
// Regular dependency update
// (Command for updating React dependencies)
npm update react
```

Executing commands like **npm update react** reflects a commitment to ongoing maintenance, ensuring that the application benefits from the latest security patches and enhancements.

In conclusion, the seamless integration of security into the Software Development Lifecycle serves as a linchpin in the creation of secure and resilient software applications. By embedding security considerations from the project's inception, adopting secure design and coding practices, implementing rigorous testing, and embracing secure deployment and maintenance measures, development teams fortify their applications against potential threats. This proactive approach not only mitigates risks but also cultivates a culture of security awareness within the software development community, fostering the creation of robust and secure digital solutions.

Chapter Five

Threat Hunting Strategies

Introduction to Threat Hunting

In the fast-changing landscape of digital security, Threat Hunting has become a proactive strategy to uncover and address potential security threats. It involves a thorough exploration of networks, systems, and logs to identify any signs of malicious activity that might evade traditional security measures. Rather than relying solely on predefined alerts, Threat Hunting entails a continuous and deliberate investigation into an organization's digital environment to detect anomalies and patterns indicative of potential threats.

A key tactic in Threat Hunting is the use of threat intelligence feeds, which offer valuable insights into the latest tactics, techniques, and procedures used by cyber adversaries. Integrating threat intelligence into the hunting process allows security analysts to tailor their searches to identify known patterns of malicious behavior. For example, in a React application, security analysts might analyze code snippets for patterns associated with common attack vectors:

```
// Code snippet under scrutiny
function handleUserInput(input) {
    // Evaluate input for potential security risks
    if (input.match(/<script>/i)) {
        // Log or flag potential cross-site scripting (XSS) attempt
```

```
    logSecurityEvent("Potential XSS Attempt", input);
}

// Further analysis and security checks...
}
```

In this React example, the code is scrutinized for the presence of a common scripting tag, serving as an indicator in the ongoing hunt for potential security threats.

Threat Hunting is not a one-size-fits-all approach; it necessitates a profound understanding of an organization's unique digital environment. Security professionals often collaborate with subject matter experts from various IT areas to gather context and insights. This collaborative approach allows for the identification of deviations from normal behavior and aids in distinguishing between benign anomalies and potential security threats.

Furthermore, Threat Hunting often involves correlating diverse data sources. Security analysts examine logs, network traffic, endpoint data, and other telemetry to create a comprehensive view of the digital landscape. This holistic analysis enables them to identify patterns or anomalies that may not be evident when examining individual data sources in isolation.

The integration of Threat Hunting into an organization's cybersecurity strategy provides several advantages. It allows for the identification of threats that may not be detectable by automated systems alone and enables organizations to stay ahead of emerging threats by proactively adapting their defenses based on the evolving tactics of cyber adversaries.

In conclusion, Threat Hunting represents a shift in cybersecurity strategy. It embodies a proactive and offensive approach, emphasizing the need to actively seek out potential threats within an organization's digital infrastructure. By leveraging threat intelligence, collaborating across IT domains, and correlating diverse data sources, security professionals can identify and mitigate potential security risks before they escalate into critical incidents. In the dynamic and constantly changing landscape of cybersecurity, Threat Hunting stands as a vital practice to strengthen the resilience of digital defenses.

Leveraging Threat Intelligence for Proactive Defense

In the dynamic arena of cybersecurity, the strategic incorporation of Threat Intelligence stands out as a linchpin for proactive defense. This approach entails harnessing comprehensive insights into the latest cyber threats, tactics, and vulnerabilities, allowing organizations to fortify their defenses against potential risks.

Threat Intelligence serves as a sentinel, constantly monitoring the digital landscape for emerging threats and providing valuable data to inform preemptive security measures. By integrating Threat Intelligence feeds into security operations, organizations gain a proactive edge in anticipating and mitigating potential cyber threats before they manifest into critical security incidents.

A key aspect of leveraging Threat Intelligence involves correlating this intelligence with existing security data to identify potential patterns or anomalies indicative of malicious activity. This correlation aids in distinguishing normal network behavior from potential security threats. For instance, within a React application, security analysts may employ code analysis to detect patterns associated with known attack vectors:

```
// React code snippet undergoing analysis
function handleUserInput(input) {
  // Scrutinizing input for potential security risks
  if (input.match(/<script>/i)) {
    // Logging or flagging potential cross-site scripting (XSS) attempt
    logSecurityEvent("Potential XSS Attempt", input);
  }

  // Additional security analysis...
}
```

In this React example, the code is analyzed for the presence of a common scripting tag, aligning with Threat Intelligence insights to proactively detect potential cross-site scripting (XSS) attempts.

Threat Intelligence also plays a crucial role in enhancing incident response capabilities. By having a preemptive understanding of likely attack scenarios, organizations can formulate response plans tailored to specific threats. This proactive stance streamlines the incident response process, enabling organizations to contain and mitigate security incidents swiftly.

Furthermore, Threat Intelligence aids in the identification of indicators of compromise (IoCs), which are crucial artifacts that signal potential security incidents. Incorporating IoCs into security monitoring processes allows organizations to actively hunt for these indicators within their network, uncovering potential threats early in their lifecycle. For example, within a React-based application, security analysts might utilize IoCs to enhance monitoring capabilities:

```
// React code snippet incorporating IoCs for enhanced monitoring
function monitorNetworkTraffic() {
  // Incorporating known IoCs for proactive threat detection
  const knownIoCs = getKnownIoCs();
  analyzeNetworkTraffic(knownIoCs);
}

function analyzeNetworkTraffic(knownIoCs) {
  // Analyzing network traffic with known IoCs
  // ...

  // Proactive threat detection and response...
}
```

In this React example, the code illustrates the integration of known IoCs into the analysis of network traffic, enhancing proactive threat detection capabilities.

Collaboration within the cybersecurity community is pivotal for effective Threat Intelligence utilization. Sharing anonymized threat data and insights among organizations bolsters the collective defense against cyber threats. Open-source Threat Intelligence platforms and Information Sharing and Analysis Centers (ISACs) facilitate this collaborative exchange, ensuring a broader and more effective defense posture.

In conclusion, leveraging Threat Intelligence for proactive defense is a strategic imperative in the contemporary cybersecurity landscape. It empowers organizations to anticipate, detect, and respond to potential cyber threats before they escalate. By integrating Threat Intelligence feeds, correlating insights with security data, and utilizing IoCs for enhanced monitoring, organizations can fortify their defenses and stay ahead of evolving cyber threats. This proactive approach is not just a defensive tactic but a strategic advantage in the ongoing battle against cyber adversaries.

Practical Threat Hunting Techniques

In the dynamic and swiftly evolving arena of cybersecurity, acquiring proficiency in practical Threat Hunting techniques becomes essential for organizations aiming to enhance their security stance. Threat Hunting goes beyond conventional security practices, demanding a proactive strategy to identify and neutralize potential threats before they escalate into critical incidents.

A valuable technique in Threat Hunting involves analyzing logs and system events. By scrutinizing logs from diverse sources like servers, firewalls, and applications, security analysts can uncover abnormal patterns or anomalies indicating potential malicious activity. For example, within a React application, examining server logs could unveil unusual patterns in user authentication:

```
// React code snippet scrutinizing authentication logs
function analyzeAuthenticationLogs() {
  const authenticationLogs = getAuthenticationLogs();

  authenticationLogs.forEach(log => {
    // Detect anomalies or suspicious patterns
    if (log.failedAttempts > 3) {
      // Raise awareness on potential brute force attack
      logSecurityEvent("Potential Brute Force Attack", log);
    }
  });

  // Further analysis and proactive threat detection...
}
```

In this React example, the code assesses authentication logs, flagging potential brute force attacks based on an unusual number of failed attempts.

Behavioral analysis stands as another key technique in Threat Hunting. By establishing a baseline of normal user behavior, security analysts can identify deviations indicative of compromised accounts or malicious activity. This involves monitoring user activities and scrutinizing deviations from established norms. For instance, within a React-based application, tracking user activity patterns could uncover suspicious behavior:

```
// React code snippet for tracking user activity
function trackUserActivity(userId, activityType) {
  const userActivity = getUserActivity(userId);

  // Analyze user activity for anomalies
  if (isSuspiciousActivity(userActivity, activityType)) {
    // Highlight potential malicious behavior
    logSecurityEvent("Potential Malicious Activity", { userId, activityType });
  }

  // Additional analysis and proactive threat detection...
}
```

Here, the React code tracks user activity and raises alerts for potential malicious behavior based on predefined criteria.

Threat intelligence integration plays a pivotal role in practical Threat Hunting. By tapping into external threat intelligence feeds, security analysts enrich their understanding of emerging threats and tailor their hunting techniques accordingly. This includes incorporating known indicators of compromise (IoCs) into the analysis process. In a React application, integrating IoCs could enhance proactive threat detection:

```
// React code snippet incorporating known IoCs
function monitorNetworkTraffic() {
  const knownIoCs = getKnownIoCs();
  const networkTraffic = getNetworkTraffic();

  // Analyze network traffic with known IoCs
  networkTraffic.forEach(packet => {
    if (matchesKnownIoC(packet, knownIoCs)) {
      // Raise awareness on potential security threat
      logSecurityEvent("Potential Security Threat", packet);
    }
  });

  // Further analysis and proactive threat detection...
}
```

In this React example, the code integrates known IoCs into the analysis of network traffic, improving the detection of potential security threats.

Effective Threat Hunting relies on collaboration among security professionals. Sharing insights, indicators, and hunting techniques within the cybersecurity community enhances the collective defense against evolving threats. Platforms such as Information Sharing and Analysis Centers

(ISACs) facilitate this collaborative exchange, fostering a more resilient cybersecurity stance.

In conclusion, acquiring proficiency in practical Threat Hunting techniques is crucial for the proactive defense against cyber threats. By analyzing logs, employing behavioral analysis, integrating threat intelligence, and fostering collaboration, organizations can fortify their security stance and stay ahead of evolving threats. Practical Threat Hunting is not just a skill; it is a strategic approach that empowers organizations to actively seek and neutralize potential threats before they escalate.

Building and Managing Threat Hunting Teams

In the rapidly changing and dynamic sphere of cybersecurity, forming and overseeing proficient Threat Hunting teams is pivotal for organizations looking to fortify their security defenses. The success of these teams hinges on a blend of skilled professionals, streamlined processes, and a collaborative environment fostering proactive threat detection and mitigation.

A fundamental aspect of constructing a Threat Hunting team is assembling a diverse set of skills. The team should consist of individuals with expertise in network security, system administration, incident response, and proficiency in tools used for log analysis and threat intelligence integration. For example, within a React-based system, the team may include specialists with skills in code analysis and behavioral tracking:

```
// React code snippet for code analysis
function examineCodeForThreats(code) {
  // Implement code analysis techniques for potential
threats
  // ...

  // Log or flag potential security risks
  logSecurityEvent("Code Analysis Result", code);
}

// React code snippet for tracking user behavior
function monitorUserBehavior(userId, activityType) {
  // Implement behavioral tracking to identify anomalies
  // ...

  // Log or flag potential malicious activity
  logSecurityEvent("User Behavior Analysis", { userId,
activityType });
}
```

In this React example, the team's expertise may involve analyzing code for potential threats and tracking user behavior to identify anomalies.

Effective communication and collaboration within the Threat Hunting team are paramount. Establishing a clear communication framework ensures that team members can efficiently share insights, findings, and collaborate on complex investigations. Utilizing collaboration tools and maintaining open lines of communication facilitates the seamless exchange of information. For instance, within a React-based collaboration tool:

```
// React code snippet for a collaboration tool
function shareThreatIntelInsights(message, channel) {
  // Utilize the collaboration tool to share threat intelligence insights
  // ...

  // Ensure a streamlined exchange of information among team members
  communicateSecurityEvent(message, channel);
}
```

In this React example, the team utilizes a collaboration tool to share threat intelligence insights and ensure effective communication.

Continuous training and skill development are integral components of managing a Threat Hunting team. Given the dynamic nature of cyber threats, staying abreast of the latest techniques and tools is imperative. The team should engage in regular training sessions, workshops, and participate in industry conferences to enhance their skills and stay informed about emerging threats. For instance, a React-based training module may cover new methodologies in threat detection:

```
// React code snippet for a training module
function conductThreatHuntingWorkshop() {
    // Develop and deliver a training module on the latest
threat hunting techniques
    // ...

    // Facilitate continuous skill development within the
Threat Hunting team
    trainSecurityProfessionals();
}
```

In this React example, the team conducts a workshop to impart the latest threat hunting techniques and facilitate ongoing skill development.

Managing the workload and priorities of a Threat Hunting team requires a strategic approach. Prioritizing threats based on potential impact, actively managing incident response workflows, and integrating threat intelligence into daily operations are critical tasks. Utilizing a React-based incident management system, the team can streamline their response processes:

```
// React code snippet for an incident management system
function manageSecurityIncidents(incident, priority) {
  // Prioritize and manage security incidents based on potential impact
  // ...

  // Integrate threat intelligence insights into incident response workflows
  respondToSecurityIncident(incident, priority);
}
```

In this React example, the team employs an incident management system to prioritize and respond to security incidents, integrating threat intelligence insights into their workflow.

In conclusion, forming and overseeing proficient Threat Hunting teams involves a combination of diverse skill sets, clear communication, continuous training, and strategic management of workload and priorities. By assembling a skilled and collaborative team, organizations can proactively detect and mitigate potential cyber threats, contributing to a robust cybersecurity posture.

Furthermore, fostering a culture of adaptability and a keen awareness of emerging threats is essential for maintaining the team's agility in the face of evolving cybersecurity challenges. Through a proactive and collaborative approach, organizations can not only stay ahead of potential risks but also cultivate a resilient cybersecurity foundation.

Chapter Six

Network Security Beyond Basics

Advanced Firewall Configurations

In the constantly changing arena of cybersecurity, the configuration of firewalls with advanced settings plays a crucial role in fortifying network security. These intricate configurations surpass standard rule sets, offering a nuanced approach to safeguarding against diverse cyber threats.

One sophisticated firewall configuration involves implementing detailed access control policies. This entails setting specific rules governing the flow of network traffic based on numerous parameters, including source and destination IP addresses, ports, and protocols. This meticulous approach enhances the firewall's capability to discern and manage incoming and outgoing traffic with precision. By tailoring access control policies within a constantly evolving cybersecurity landscape, organizations can proactively strengthen their defenses against a myriad of potential threats. Within a React-based firewall management system, such rules can be exemplified as follows:

```
// React code snippet for implementing detailed access
control policies
function configureFirewallRules() {
  // Define specific rules for incoming and outgoing
traffic
  setFirewallRule({
    sourceIP: '192.168.1.0/24',
    destinationIP: '10.0.0.1',
    port: 80,
    protocol: 'TCP',
    action: 'ALLOW',
  });

  // Additional rules for different scenarios...
}
```

In this React example, the code showcases the configuration of a firewall rule that allows traffic from a specific source IP to a designated destination IP on port 80 using the TCP protocol. This level of granularity enhances the firewall's efficacy in permitting or restricting traffic based on precise criteria.

Another advanced firewall configuration involves the incorporation of Intrusion Prevention Systems (IPS). IPS operates at a deeper level than traditional firewalls, inspecting network packets for malicious content or patterns. When integrated into a React-based firewall management system, the IPS configuration might look like this:

```javascript
// React code snippet for configuring Intrusion
Prevention Systems
function configureIPS() {
  // Enable Intrusion Prevention for deep packet
inspection
  enableIntrusionPrevention();

  // Configure specific rules to detect and block known
attack patterns
  setIPSRule({
    signature: 'SQL Injection',
    action: 'BLOCK',
  });

  // Additional rules for different attack patterns...
}
```

In this React example, the code illustrates the activation of Intrusion Prevention, coupled with specific rules to identify and block known attack patterns such as SQL injection. This advanced layer of defense enhances the firewall's capability to thwart sophisticated cyber threats.

Furthermore, leveraging Virtual LANs (VLANs) within firewall configurations enhances network segmentation, bolstering security by isolating different parts of the network. A React-based VLAN configuration snippet might look like this:

```
// React code snippet for VLAN configuration within
firewalls
function configureVLANs() {
  // Create separate VLANs for different departments or
segments
  createVLAN({
    name: 'Finance',
    subnet: '192.168.2.0/24',
  });

  // Associate specific firewall rules for each VLAN
  associateFirewallRules('Finance',
getFinanceFirewallRules());

  // Additional VLAN configurations for other segments...
}
```

In this React example, the code demonstrates the creation of a VLAN for the Finance department, each with its own subnet. This approach allows organizations to apply tailored firewall rules to each VLAN, effectively isolating network segments and mitigating the impact of a potential breach.

Moreover, the integration of Stateful Packet Inspection (SPI) enhances firewall intelligence by keeping track of the state of active connections and making decisions based on the context of the traffic. In a React-based firewall management system, the SPI configuration might appear as follows:

```
// React code snippet for configuring Stateful Packet
Inspection
function configureSPI() {
  // Enable Stateful Packet Inspection for enhanced
traffic analysis
  enableSPI();

  // Define rules based on the state of active
connections
  setSPIRule({
    state: 'ESTABLISHED',
    action: 'ALLOW',
  });

  // Additional rules for different connection states...
}
```

In this React example, the code showcases the activation of Stateful Packet Inspection, coupled with rules that permit traffic based on the established state. This intelligent approach enhances the firewall's ability to discern legitimate connections from potential threats.

In conclusion, the configuration of advanced firewall settings is pivotal in establishing a robust defense against sophisticated cyber threats. By implementing granular access control, integrating Intrusion Prevention Systems, leveraging Virtual LANs for network segmentation, and incorporating Stateful Packet Inspection, organizations can enhance their network security posture. These advanced configurations, when seamlessly integrated into a React-based firewall management system, contribute to a resilient defense strategy in the ever-challenging landscape of cybersecurity.

Intrusion Detection and Prevention Systems (IDPS)

Within the ever-changing landscape of digital security, Intrusion Detection and Prevention Systems (IDPS) emerge as crucial components in fortifying an organization's defense mechanisms. These systems actively observe network and system activities, swiftly identifying and responding to potential security threats and incidents.

At the heart of an IDPS lies its ability to scrutinize network traffic and system logs, utilizing various detection mechanisms to pinpoint unusual patterns or behaviors that may indicate potential intrusions. Reacting promptly to potential threats is paramount, and within a React-based IDPS implementation, this can be exemplified through code:

```
// React code snippet for implementing IDPS anomaly detection
function analyzeNetworkTraffic() {
  // Implement algorithms for detecting anomalies in network traffic
  // ...

  // Activate response mechanisms for identified anomalies
```

```
  respondToAnomaly();
}

// React code snippet for logging security events
function logSecurityEvent(eventType, details) {
  // Record security events for further analysis and
response
  // ...

  // Maintain an audit trail of potential security
incidents
  recordSecurityEvent(eventType, details);
}
```

In this React example, the code showcases the deployment of anomaly detection algorithms on network traffic. Detected anomalies trigger response mechanisms and log security events for subsequent analysis.

A critical aspect of IDPS functionalities lies in its capabilities for intrusion detection and prevention. Detection involves identifying potential threats and notifying security personnel, while prevention goes a step further by actively obstructing or mitigating identified threats. This proactive approach is pivotal in halting potential security breaches before they can cause harm. Within a React-based IDPS implementation, this distinction can be demonstrated:

```
// React code snippet for IDPS intrusion prevention
function preventIntrusion() {
  // Implement mechanisms to actively obstruct or
mitigate identified threats
  // ...

  // Log prevented intrusion attempts for auditing
purposes
  logPreventedIntrusion();
}

// React code snippet for alerting security personnel
function notifySecurityPersonnel(message) {
  // Notify security personnel about detected threats or
intrusion attempts
  // ...

  // Ensure a timely response to potential security
incidents
  informSecurityTeam(message);
}
```

In this React example, the code displays the deployment of intrusion prevention mechanisms and the notification of security personnel about detected threats. This dual capability guarantees a swift and comprehensive response to potential security incidents.

Additionally, IDPS systems often rely on signature-based detection, where predefined patterns or signatures of known threats are compared against current network or system activity. This signature-based approach is illustrated within a React-based IDPS through the following code snippet:

```
// React code snippet for signature-based detection
function detectSignatureBasedThreats() {
  // Compare network traffic and system logs against predefined threat signatures
  // ...

  // Take appropriate action upon detecting a signature-based threat
  handleSignatureBasedThreat();
}

// React code snippet for updating threat signatures
function refreshThreatSignatures() {
  // Regularly update threat signatures to stay informed about emerging threats
  // ...

  // Ensure the IDPS system is equipped to detect the latest threat patterns
  updateThreatSignatures();
}
```

In this React example, the code demonstrates the detection of signature-based threats and the periodic update of threat signatures to stay ahead of emerging cybersecurity risks.

In conclusion, Intrusion Detection and Prevention Systems play a vital role in strengthening the security posture of organizations by actively monitoring, detecting, and responding to potential security threats. The utilization of React-based implementations, as illustrated through code snippets, underscores the technical intricacies involved in ensuring a robust defense against evolving cybersecurity challenges.

Segmentation Strategies for Enhanced Security

In the dynamic sphere of cybersecurity, the deployment of effective segmentation strategies emerges as a fundamental pillar for fortifying the security stance of an organization's network. These strategies entail the division of the network into distinct segments or zones, each endowed with its unique set of security protocols and access controls. Through this compartmentalization, organizations can mitigate the potential impact of security breaches and bolster their overall defense against cyber threats.

A fundamental strategy involves network segmentation, where the network undergoes division into isolated segments to impede lateral movements by potential attackers. Within a React-based network segmentation strategy, code can be employed to illustrate this concept:

```
// React code snippet for implementing network
segmentation
function implementNetworkSegments() {
  // Specify isolated network segments for different
departments
  createNetworkSegment('Finance', '192.168.1.0/24');
  createNetworkSegment('Research', '192.168.2.0/24');

  // Enforce access controls to restrict communication
between segments
  enforceAccessControls('Finance', 'Research');
}
```

In this React example, the code demonstrates the establishment of isolated network segments for the Finance and Research departments, each allocated its unique IP range. Access controls are then implemented to confine communication between these segments, thwarting unauthorized access and curtailing the lateral spread of potential threats.

Another pivotal segmentation strategy involves the implementation of micro-segmentation within data centers. This approach subdivides the data center into finely grained segments, enabling organizations to regulate communication between specific workloads. In a React-based implementation, this concept can be depicted through code:

```
// React code snippet for implementing data center micro-
segmentation
function implementMicroSegmentation() {
  // Create finely grained segments for different
application workloads
  createDataCenterSegment('Web Servers', '10.0.1.0/24');
  createDataCenterSegment('Database Servers', '10.0.2.0/24');

  // Define precise access rules for communication
between workloads
  defineAccessRules('Web Servers', 'Database Servers');
}
```

In this React example, the code showcases the establishment of finely grained segments for Web Servers and Database Servers within a data center. Precise access rules are then defined to govern communication between these specific workloads, diminishing the attack surface and thwarting unauthorized interactions.

Furthermore, endpoint segmentation is a vital strategy concentrating on securing individual devices within the network. By categorizing endpoints based on their roles and implementing specific security policies, organizations can enhance protection against endpoint-targeted attacks. In a React-based endpoint segmentation scenario, code can exemplify this concept:

```
// React code snippet for implementing endpoint
segmentation
function implementEndpointSegmentation() {
  // Categorize endpoints based on roles (e.g., employee
devices, servers)
  categorizeEndpoints('Employee Devices',
'192.168.10.0/24');
  categorizeEndpoints('Servers', '192.168.20.0/24');

  // Apply role-specific security policies to each
endpoint category
  applySecurityPolicies('Employee Devices', 'Servers');
}
```

In this React example, the code categorizes endpoints into Employee Devices and Servers, each assigned its unique IP range. Role-specific security policies are then applied to ensure that devices within each category adhere to the defined security protocols.

In conclusion, segmentation strategies assume a pivotal role in fortifying an organization's cybersecurity defenses by compartmentalizing the network into distinct segments. Whether through network segmentation, data center micro-segmentation, or endpoint segmentation, the utilization of React-based implementations, as illustrated through code snippets, underscores the technical intricacies involved in enhancing security through strategic segmentation. These strategies collectively contribute to minimizing the attack surface and controlling communication flows, ultimately bolstering the resilience of an organization's cybersecurity infrastructure.

Secure Configuration Management

In the dynamic and evolving arena of cybersecurity, a fundamental element in fortifying defenses is the practice of Secure Configuration Management. This discipline revolves around the meticulous configuration and upkeep of security settings for hardware, software, and network components, aiming to minimize vulnerabilities and ensure the secure operation of systems.

Within the scope of secure configuration management, the proper configuration of software components takes precedence. Consider the following React-based code snippet as an illustration of secure configurations:

```
// React code snippet for ensuring the secure
configuration of a web server
function configureWebServer() {
  // Establish secure HTTP response headers
  setHTTPHeaders({
    'Strict-Transport-Security': 'max-age=31536000; includeSubDomains',
    'X-Content-Type-Options': 'nosniff',
    'X-Frame-Options': 'DENY',
    'Content-Security-Policy': 'default-src https:; script-src https:',
  });

  // Set up secure communication settings
```

```
setSSLSettings({
  key: 'path/to/private.key',
  cert: 'path/to/certificate.crt',
});

// Implement additional secure configuration settings...
}
```

In this React example, the code showcases the secure configuration of a web server, incorporating stringent HTTP response headers and secure communication settings. These measures contribute to averting common web vulnerabilities and ensuring the confidentiality and integrity of data in transit.

Secure configuration management also extends its reach to network devices, where misconfigurations can pose potential security risks. In a React-based network device configuration snippet:

```
// React code snippet for ensuring the secure configuration of a network device
function configureNetworkDevice() {
  // Define access control lists to restrict unauthorized access
  setAccessControlLists({
    inbound: 'deny from any to 10.0.0.1',
    outbound: 'allow from 10.0.0.1 to any',
```

```
});

// Configure secure management settings
setManagementSettings({
  enableSSH: true,
  enableHTTPS: true,
});

// Implement additional secure configuration settings...
}
```

In this React example, the code emphasizes the secure configuration of a network device by incorporating access control lists to limit unauthorized access and configuring secure management settings. These measures assist in averting unauthorized network access and securing the device's management interfaces.

Moreover, secure configuration management encompasses the establishment of secure baseline configurations for operating systems. In a React-based operating system configuration snippet:

```js
// React code snippet for ensuring the secure
configuration of an operating
system
function configureOperatingSystem() {
  // Set account lockout policies to deter brute force
attacks
  setAccountLockoutPolicy({
    maxFailedAttempts: 5,
    lockoutDuration: '15 minutes',
  });

  // Configure secure password policies
  setPasswordPolicy({
    minimumLength: 12,
    requireSpecialCharacters: true,
    requireNumbers: true,
  });

  // Implement additional secure configuration
settings...
}
```

In this React example, the code establishes account lockout policies and secure password policies for an operating system. These measures enhance the security of user accounts and discourage unauthorized access attempts.

Secure configuration management is an ongoing process that necessitates regular reviews and updates. Automated tools can assist in maintaining secure configurations and ensuring compliance with security policies. In a React-based automated configuration management snippet:

```
// React code snippet for automated checks on secure
configurations
function automateSecureConfigurationChecks() {
  // Employ configuration management tools for checking
and enforcing secure settings
  automateUsingTool('SecureConfigChecker');

  // Schedule routine automated scans for configuration
vulnerabilities
  scheduleAutomatedScans('Weekly',
'SecureConfigScanner');
}
```

In this React example, the code underscores the use of configuration management tools to automate the verification and enforcement of secure settings. Scheduled automated scans help identify and rectify any configuration vulnerabilities that may arise over time.

In conclusion, secure configuration management is a critical facet of cybersecurity, ensuring that systems are configured securely to mitigate potential vulnerabilities. Whether configuring software components, network devices, operating systems, or leveraging automated tools, the emphasis on secure configurations is indispensable for building a robust defense against evolving cybersecurity threats.

Chapter Seven

Advanced Cryptography

Cryptographic Protocols and Algorithms

In the ever-advancing field of cybersecurity, the implementation of robust cryptographic protocols and algorithms plays a pivotal role in safeguarding sensitive information and ensuring the integrity of data transmissions. Cryptography, as an essential component of secure communication, relies on sophisticated protocols and algorithms to encrypt and decrypt information, shielding it from unauthorized access or manipulation.

Within the realm of cryptographic protocols, a fundamental cornerstone is the Transport Layer Security (TLS) protocol, which secures communication over networks. In a React-based context, consider the following code snippet illustrating the implementation of TLS:

```
// React code snippet for implementing TLS in a web server
function implementTLS() {
  // Configure TLS settings
  setTLSSettings({
    version: 'TLSv1.3',
    ciphers: ['TLS_AES_128_GCM_SHA256', 'TLS_AES_256_GCM_SHA384'],
    keyExchange: 'ECDHE',
  });
```

```
// Enable TLS in the web server
enableTLS();
}
```

In this React example, the code demonstrates the configuration of TLS settings, specifying the version, ciphers, and key exchange mechanism. Enabling TLS in the web server ensures secure communication by encrypting data during transit, thwarting potential eavesdropping or tampering.

Asymmetric cryptography, another integral aspect of cryptographic protocols, employs key pairs for encryption and decryption. The following React-based code snippet showcases the generation of an asymmetric key pair:

```
// React code snippet for generating an asymmetric key pair
function generateAsymmetricKeyPair() {
  // Generate a public-private key pair
  const keyPair = generateKeyPair('RSA', {
    modulusLength: 2048,
    publicKeyEncoding: {
      type: 'spki',
      format: 'pem',
    },
    privateKeyEncoding: {
      type: 'pkcs8',
      format: 'pem',
```

```
    },
  });

  // Store the key pair securely
  storeKeyPair(keyPair);
}
```

In this React example, the code generates an RSA key pair with a specified modulus length and encoding format. The resulting public-private key pair is then stored securely, ready to be utilized for secure communication and data integrity verification.

Hash functions, a crucial element in cryptographic algorithms, ensure the integrity of data by producing a fixed-size hash value. The following React-based code snippet exemplifies the application of a hash function:

```
// React code snippet for hashing data
function hashData(data) {
  // Apply a secure hash function (e.g., SHA-256) to the data
  const hashedData = hash('sha256', data);

  // Verify integrity by comparing hash values
  verifyIntegrity(hashedData);
}
```

In this React example, the code utilizes the SHA-256 hash function to hash data securely. Verifying integrity involves comparing hash values to ensure that the data has not been altered during transmission or storage.

Furthermore, the Advanced Encryption Standard (AES), a widely adopted symmetric encryption algorithm, ensures confidentiality through the use of a shared key. Here's a React-based code snippet showcasing the application of AES encryption:

```
// React code snippet for AES encryption
function encryptData(data, key) {
  // Use AES encryption with a specified key
  const encryptedData = encrypt('aes-256-cbc', key, data);

  // Ensure only authorized parties can decrypt the data
  authorizeDecryption(encryptedData);
}
```

In this React example, the code encrypts data using the AES-256-CBC algorithm with a specified key, ensuring that only entities with the authorized decryption key can decipher the information.

In conclusion, cryptographic protocols and algorithms are instrumental in fortifying cybersecurity measures, providing a robust framework for secure communication and data protection. Whether implementing TLS for secure network communication, generating asymmetric key pairs, applying hash functions for data integrity, or utilizing symmetric encryption like AES, the application of these cryptographic components exemplifies the technical intricacies involved in ensuring the confidentiality, integrity, and authenticity of digital information.

Implementing Secure Key Management

The establishment of secure key management practices emerges as a crucial element in preserving the confidentiality of sensitive information. Key management, a cornerstone in cryptographic systems, involves the meticulous handling of cryptographic keys, encompassing their secure generation, distribution, storage, and eventual disposal.

One fundamental aspect of secure key management entails the generation of cryptographic keys through reliable algorithms. Illustrated through a React-based code snippet, the process of generating an asymmetric key pair using the RSA algorithm can be demonstrated:

```
// React code snippet for creating an asymmetric key pair (RSA)
function generateSecureKeyPair() {
  // Produce a secure public-private key pair
  const keyPair = generateKeyPair('RSA', {
    modulusLength: 2048,
    publicKeyEncoding: {
      type: 'spki',
      format: 'pem',
    },
    privateKeyEncoding: {
```

```
    type: 'pkcs8',
    format: 'pem',
  },
});

// Store the resulting key pair securely
storeSecureKeyPair(keyPair);
}
```

In this React example, the code employs the RSA algorithm to generate a secure public-private key pair with a specified modulus length. The ensuing keys are then securely stored for subsequent cryptographic operations.

Another critical facet is the secure distribution of cryptographic keys, ensuring their sharing exclusively among authorized entities. Through React, the code snippet below exemplifies a secure key distribution process:

```
// React code snippet for securely distributing
cryptographic keys
function distributeSecureKey(key, recipient) {
  // Encrypt the cryptographic key for the intended
recipient
  const encryptedKey = encrypt('aes-256-cbc',
recipient.publicKey, key);

  // Transmit the encrypted key securely to the recipient
  ensureSecureTransmission(encryptedKey, recipient);
}
```

In this React example, the code encrypts a cryptographic key using the recipient's public key before securely transmitting it. This process guarantees the confidentiality of the key during distribution, ensuring that only the intended recipient can decipher and utilize it.

Effective key storage mechanisms are imperative to prevent unauthorized access to cryptographic keys. Adopting secure storage practices, as demonstrated in the React code snippet below, adds an extra layer of protection:

```
// React code snippet for securely storing cryptographic
keys
function storeSecureKey(key) {
  // Utilize a secure key vault or hardware security
module (HSM) for storage
  secureStorageUtil.storeKey(key);
}
```

In this React example, the code underscores the use of secure key vaults or hardware security modules (HSMs) for storing cryptographic keys. These dedicated and fortified storage solutions enhance overall security by shielding keys from unauthorized access.

The secure disposal of cryptographic keys at the conclusion of their lifecycle is paramount to mitigate the risk of unauthorized usage. In a React-based code snippet, the process of securely deleting a cryptographic key is illustrated:

```
// React code snippet for securely disposing of
cryptographic keys
function securelyDisposeOfKey(key) {
  // Overwrite the key material with random data before
deletion
  overwriteAndDeleteKeyMaterial(key);
}
```

In this React example, the code emphasizes the secure disposal of cryptographic keys by overwriting the key material with random data before initiating the deletion process. This practice reduces the likelihood of recovering sensitive key information after deletion.

In conclusion, the implementation of secure key management practices is an indispensable element in fortifying cybersecurity defenses. Whether generating cryptographic keys, securely distributing them, employing robust storage mechanisms, or ensuring their secure disposal, the application of these practices, as exemplified through React code snippets, underscores the technical intricacies involved in safeguarding cryptographic key infrastructure. Adhering collectively to these principles contributes to a resilient cybersecurity framework, protecting sensitive data and ensuring the integrity of cryptographic operations.

Securing Communications with SSL/TLS

Ensuring the confidentiality and integrity of communications stands as a paramount concern. One crucial method employed for this purpose is the implementation of Secure Socket Layer (SSL) and its successor, Transport Layer Security (TLS) protocols. These protocols establish encrypted connections between communicating parties, thereby fortifying data transmission against eavesdropping, tampering, or unauthorized access.

Within the context of web development, the act of securing communications using SSL/TLS is essential for safeguarding sensitive information exchanged between users and web servers. A practical illustration in React showcases the steps involved in configuring SSL/TLS for a web server:

```
// React code snippet for setting up SSL/TLS in a web
server
function setupSSLTLS() {
  // Load SSL/TLS certificate and private key
  const certificate = loadCertificate('path/to/certificate.crt');
  const privateKey = loadPrivateKey('path/to/private.key');

  // Configure the web server with SSL/TLS settings
  configureServerWithSSL({
    certificate,
    privateKey,
    protocol: 'TLSv1.3',
    ciphers: ['TLS_AES_128_GCM_SHA256', 'TLS_AES_256_GCM_SHA384'],
  });

  // Start the server with SSL/TLS support
  commenceServerWithSSL();
}
```

In this React example, the code encompasses the essential steps in setting up SSL/TLS for a web server. It involves loading the SSL/TLS certificate and private key, specifying the desired protocol version (TLSv1.3), and defining acceptable ciphers for secure communication.

Moreover, SSL/TLS plays a pivotal role in securing communication over APIs. In a React-based API communication example:

```
// React code snippet for secure API communication using SSL/TLS
function communicateWithSecuredAPI() {
  // Establish a secure connection to the API server
  const secureConnection = establishSecureConnection('api.example.com', {
    protocol: 'TLSv1.2',
    ciphers: ['TLS_AES_128_GCM_SHA256'],
  });

  // Send secure requests and receive encrypted responses
  const secureResponse = sendSecureRequest(secureConnection, '/endpoint', 'GET');

  // Process the secure response
  handleSecureResponse(secureResponse);
}
```

In this React example, the code underscores the importance of specifying the protocol version and accepted ciphers when establishing a secure connection to an API server. This ensures that the API communication is encrypted, enhancing the confidentiality of transmitted data.

Beyond web and API scenarios, securing email communications is another critical application of SSL/TLS. In a React-based email configuration snippet:

```js
// React code snippet for configuring SSL/TLS for email communication
function setupEmailWithSSL() {
  // Load SSL/TLS certificate and private key for the email server
  const emailCertificate = loadCertificate('path/to/email-certificate.crt');
  const emailPrivateKey = loadPrivateKey('path/to/email-private.key');

  // Configure email client with SSL/TLS settings
  configureEmailClientWithSSL({
    certificate: emailCertificate,
    privateKey: emailPrivateKey,
    protocol: 'TLSv1.2',
    ciphers: ['TLS_AES_128_GCM_SHA256'],
  });

  // Connect to the email server securely
  establishSecureConnectionToEmailServer();
}
```

In this React example, the code illustrates the configuration of SSL/TLS for an email client, emphasizing the importance of loading the appropriate certificate and private key for establishing a secure connection to the email server.

The secure transmission of data over the internet is a foundational aspect of modern digital security. Implementing SSL/TLS protocols, as demonstrated through React code snippets, underscores the practical steps involved in configuring secure connections for web servers, APIs, and email communication. By adopting these measures, organizations and developers contribute to a safer online environment, mitigating risks associated with unauthorized access and data breaches during the exchange of sensitive information.

Cryptography in Blockchain Technology

cryptography emerges as a crucial element ensuring the security and integrity of data, particularly in the context of Blockchain technology. Cryptography plays a pivotal role in providing the foundation for the secure and trustless nature of Blockchain systems, contributing to their widespread adoption and application across diverse industries.

At its core, Blockchain is a decentralized and distributed ledger that records transactions across a network of computers in a secure and transparent manner. The utilization of cryptographic techniques within Blockchain serves to address key challenges such as ensuring the immutability of data, securing transactions, and validating the authenticity of participants.

A fundamental application of cryptography in Blockchain is the creation and verification of digital signatures. Digital signatures authenticate the origin and integrity of data within a block, preventing malicious alterations. In a React-based example, the following code snippet illustrates the process of generating and verifying a digital signature:

```js
// React code snippet for digital signature generation and verification
function generateDigitalSignature(data, privateKey) {
  // Use a cryptographic library to sign the data with a private key
  const signature = signData(data, privateKey);

  // Append the generated signature to the data block
  const signedData = { data, signature };

  return signedData;
}

function verifyDigitalSignature(signedData, publicKey) {
  // Extract the signature and data from the signed block
  const { data, signature } = signedData;

  // Use the public key to verify the signature
  const isSignatureValid = verifySignature(data, signature, publicKey);

  return isSignatureValid;
}
```

In this React example, the code showcases the creation of a digital signature for data using a private key and the subsequent verification of that signature using the corresponding public key. This process ensures the integrity and authenticity of the information stored in a Blockchain block. Another critical cryptographic aspect in Blockchain is the use of hash functions. Hash functions create a fixed-size output (hash) for any input data, providing a unique identifier for each block. React code can illustrate the hashing process within a Blockchain:

```
// React code snippet for hash function usage in Blockchain
function calculateHash(data) {
  // Apply a cryptographic hash function to the data
  const hash = hashData(data);

  return hash;
}
```

In this React example, the code applies a hash function to the data within a block, generating a fixed-size hash that uniquely represents the block's contents. This hash is crucial for maintaining the integrity of the Blockchain by linking blocks together.

Encryption also plays a role in preserving the confidentiality of sensitive data within a Blockchain. For instance, in a React-based snippet:

```
// React code snippet for encrypting and decrypting data
in Blockchain
function encryptData(data, publicKey) {
  // Use asymmetric encryption to encrypt the data with a
public key
  const encryptedData = encryptWithPublicKey(data,
publicKey);

  return encryptedData;
}

function decryptData(encryptedData, privateKey) {
  // Use the corresponding private key to decrypt the
data
  const decryptedData =
decryptWithPrivateKey(encryptedData, privateKey);

  return decryptedData;
}
```

This React code exemplifies the use of asymmetric encryption to protect sensitive data. It encrypts data with a recipient's public key, ensuring that only the possessor of the corresponding private key can decrypt and access the original information.

The symbiotic relationship between cryptography and Blockchain technology underscores the robust security foundations that facilitate trust and transparency in decentralized systems. From digital signatures and hash functions to encryption, cryptographic techniques are integral in shaping the secure and reliable nature of Blockchain networks. As the technology continues to evolve, the fusion of cryptography and Blockchain will remain a cornerstone in building resilient and trustworthy decentralized ecosystems.

Chapter Eight

Cloud Security Best Practices

Navigating Cloud Security Challenges

In the continually shifting area of cloud computing, ensuring robust security measures remains a paramount concern for organizations leveraging cloud services. As businesses increasingly migrate their operations to cloud environments, they encounter a spectrum of security challenges that demand careful navigation to safeguard sensitive data and maintain the integrity of their digital infrastructure.

One significant challenge in cloud security is the shared responsibility model. Cloud service providers, like AWS or Azure, offer a shared responsibility framework where they manage the security of the cloud infrastructure, while customers are responsible for securing their data within the cloud. A React code snippet exemplifies how organizations can enhance their security within this shared responsibility model:

```
// React code snippet for implementing security within the shared responsibility model
function implementSecurityInSharedModel() {
  // Leverage cloud provider tools for securing infrastructure
  const secureInfrastructure = useCloudProviderSecurityTools();
```

```
// Implement data encryption and access controls for
sensitive information
  encryptSensitiveData();
  applyAccessControls();

// Regularly audit and monitor cloud resources for
security compliance
  performSecurityAudits();
  monitorSecurityMetrics();
}
```

This React example encapsulates actions organizations can take within the shared responsibility model, including using native security tools provided by the cloud provider, implementing encryption for sensitive data, applying access controls, and conducting regular security audits and monitoring.

Another significant challenge is the dynamic nature of cloud environments, where resources can be rapidly provisioned and de-provisioned. This dynamism introduces the need for continuous security monitoring and automation. A React-based code snippet illustrates the concept of automated security checks within a cloud environment:

```
// React code snippet for automated security checks in a
dynamic cloud
environment
function automateSecurityChecks() {
  // Implement automated security scans for new and
modified resources
  automateResourceScans();

  // Utilize continuous monitoring tools to detect and
respond to security incidents
  implementContinuousMonitoring();
  respondToSecurityIncidents();
}
```

In this React example, the code emphasizes the importance of automating security checks for newly provisioned or modified resources in a dynamic cloud environment. Continuous monitoring tools are employed to detect and respond to security incidents in real-time. Identity and access management (IAM) complexities represent another cloud security challenge. With numerous users, roles, and permissions, organizations must meticulously manage access controls. A React-based code snippet showcases how IAM can be effectively handled:

```
// React code snippet for effective Identity and Access
Management in the cloud
function manageIAM() {
  // Implement role-based access controls (RBAC) for
users and resources
  implementRBAC();

  // Enforce the principle of least privilege to limit
user access
  enforceLeastPrivilege();

  // Regularly review and audit IAM policies for accuracy
and relevance
  reviewAndAuditIAMPolicies();
}
```

In this React example, the code outlines the implementation of role-based access controls (RBAC), the enforcement of the principle of least privilege, and regular reviews and audits of IAM policies to ensure accuracy and relevance.

Data privacy and compliance with regulatory standards also loom large in cloud security concerns. Organizations must navigate a complex landscape of regulations, such as GDPR or HIPAA, to safeguard customer data. A React-based code snippet illustrates actions for ensuring data privacy and compliance:

```
// React code snippet for ensuring data privacy and
compliance in the cloud
function ensureDataPrivacyAndCompliance() {
  // Implement data encryption in transit and at rest
  encryptDataInTransit();
  encryptDataAtRest();

  // Regularly conduct compliance assessments and audits
  conductComplianceAssessments();
  performRegularAudits();
}
```

In this React example, the code emphasizes the implementation of data encryption measures, both in transit and at rest, as well as regular compliance assessments and audits to adhere to regulatory standards.

Navigating cloud security challenges demands a multifaceted approach that combines leveraging cloud provider tools, implementing automation for continuous monitoring, effectively managing IAM complexities, and ensuring data privacy and compliance. The dynamic nature of cloud environments necessitates a proactive stance, with organizations embracing security measures that evolve in tandem with their cloud infrastructure. Adopting these practices enables organizations to harness the benefits of the cloud while maintaining the highest standards of security and compliance.

Secure Cloud Configuration and Management

Ensuring the secure configuration and effective management of cloud resources emerge as pivotal elements in upholding a robust cybersecurity strategy. Organizations leveraging cloud services find themselves navigating a landscape where the complexities of configuration settings can either fortify or compromise the security posture of their digital infrastructure. Guaranteeing secure cloud configuration and management involves the adoption of best practices, the deployment of automation, and maintaining a vigilant stance against the ever-changing panorama of emerging threats.

A foundational aspect of secure cloud configuration revolves around the meticulous management of access controls and permissions. In a React code snippet, organizations can illustrate the implementation of the principle of least privilege to restrict user access:

```
// React code snippet for implementing the principle of
least privilege in cloud
access controls
function enforceLeastPrivilegeInCloud() {
  // Establish IAM policies delineating the minimum
necessary permissions for each user or role
  const userPolicy = createLeastPrivilegePolicy();

  // Apply policies to guarantee users have access only
to indispensable resources
  applyLeastPrivilegePolicy(userPolicy);
}
```

In this React example, the code underscores the creation and application of IAM policies that grant users and roles the minimum necessary permissions, aligning with the principle of least privilege. This mitigates the risk of unauthorized access and potential security breaches. The automation of cloud configurations stands out as another fundamental aspect of a secure cloud environment. Continuous integration and continuous deployment (CI/CD) pipelines prove instrumental in automating the provisioning and updating of cloud resources. A React-based code snippet illustrates the automation of cloud configurations:

```
// React code snippet for automating cloud configurations
using CI/CD pipelines
function automateCloudConfigurations() {
  // Integrate cloud infrastructure as code into CI/CD
pipelines
  integrateInfrastructureAsCode();

  // Automate the deployment and updates of cloud
resources
  automateDeploymentProcesses();
}
```

In this React example, the code showcases the integration of cloud infrastructure as code into CI/CD pipelines, streamlining the automation of deployment and updates for cloud resources. This approach enhances efficiency while minimizing the likelihood of manual configuration errors.

Encryption assumes a pivotal role in securing data in transit and at rest within the cloud environment. The implementation of encryption protocols can be exemplified in a React code snippet:

```
// React code snippet for implementing encryption in cloud data storage
function implementCloudEncryption() {
  // Utilize TLS/SSL protocols for encrypting data in transit
  encryptDataInTransit();

  // Implement encryption mechanisms for securing data at rest in cloud storage
  encryptDataAtRest();
}
```

In this React example, the code emphasizes the utilization of TLS/SSL protocols to encrypt data during transit and the implementation of encryption mechanisms to secure data at rest within cloud storage. This ensures that sensitive information remains protected from unauthorized access.

Regular auditing and monitoring of cloud configurations are imperative to identify and rectify potential security vulnerabilities promptly. React-based code can exemplify the implementation of continuous monitoring processes:

```
// React code snippet for continuous auditing and
monitoring of cloud
configurations
function continuousCloudMonitoring() {
  // Implement automated tools to regularly scan and
audit cloud configurations
  implementAutomatedAuditing();

  // Set up real-time monitoring for identifying and
responding to security incidents
  establishRealTimeMonitoring();
}
```

In this React example, the code underscores the use of automated tools for regular scanning and auditing of cloud configurations, coupled with real-time monitoring capabilities to swiftly identify and respond to potential security incidents.

In conclusion, ensuring the secure configuration of cloud resources and their effective management demands a proactive and multifaceted approach. By implementing the principle of least privilege, automating configuration processes, employing encryption measures, and establishing continuous auditing and monitoring, organizations can fortify their cloud security posture. In the ever-changing realm of cloud computing, embracing these practices ensures that organizations are well-equipped to navigate the intricacies and emerging threats associated with secure cloud configuration and management.

Identity and Access Management in the Cloud

The careful oversight of identity and access assumes a pivotal role in shaping the security stance of organizations. As businesses progressively transition their operations to cloud environments, the challenges linked to controlling user access and permissions become more pronounced. Establishing robust Identity and Access Management (IAM) practices in the cloud is essential for ensuring the confidentiality, integrity, and availability of sensitive data.

IAM in the cloud involves defining and controlling the roles and permissions assigned to users, ensuring that individuals have the appropriate level of access to resources. In a React code snippet, organizations can showcase the implementation of role-based access controls (RBAC) to streamline user management:

```
// React code snippet for implementing Role-Based Access Controls (RBAC) in cloud IAM
function implementRBACInCloudIAM() {
  // Define roles with specific permissions for different categories of users
  const adminRole = createAdminRole();
  const userRole = createUserRole();

  // Assign roles to users based on their responsibilities
  assignRoleToUser(adminRole, "AdminUser");
  assignRoleToUser(userRole, "RegularUser");
}
```

In this React example, the code demonstrates the creation of roles, such as admin and user, each with distinct permissions. Users are then assigned roles based on their responsibilities, adhering to the principle of least privilege to limit access to necessary resources.

IAM in the cloud extends beyond user roles, encompassing the principle of least privilege to minimize the potential impact of a security breach. A React code snippet can illustrate the enforcement of least privilege to restrict user access to the bare minimum necessary:

```
// React code snippet for enforcing the Principle of
Least Privilege in cloud IAM
function enforceLeastPrivilegeInCloudIAM() {
  // Implement policies to grant users the minimum
required permissions for their tasks
  const userPolicy = createLeastPrivilegePolicy();

  // Apply policies to ensure users have access only to
indispensable resources
  applyLeastPrivilegePolicy(userPolicy);
}
```

In this React example, the code emphasizes the creation and application of policies that grant users the minimum necessary permissions, reducing the risk of unauthorized access and potential security incidents.

IAM in the cloud also involves managing the lifecycle of user identities, including onboarding, changes in roles, and offboarding. A React-based code snippet can showcase the automation of user identity lifecycle management:

```
// React code snippet for automating user identity
lifecycle management in cloud
IAM
function automateIdentityLifecycleManagement() {
  // Integrate identity lifecycle management into CI/CD
pipelines
  integrateIdentityLifecycleManagement();

  // Automate onboarding, role changes, and offboarding
processes
  automateOnboarding();
  automateRoleChanges();
  automateOffboarding();
}
```

In this React example, the code illustrates the integration of identity lifecycle management into CI/CD pipelines, streamlining processes related to onboarding, role changes, and offboarding. Automation enhances efficiency and reduces the likelihood of manual errors during identity management.

Security auditing and monitoring are integral components of IAM in the cloud, allowing organizations to detect and respond to anomalous activities promptly. A React-based code snippet can exemplify the implementation of continuous monitoring:

```
// React code snippet for continuous auditing and
monitoring of cloud IAM
function continuousCloudIAMMonitoring() {
  // Implement automated tools to regularly scan and
audit IAM policies
  implementAutomatedAuditing();

  // Set up real-time monitoring for identifying and
responding to security incidents
  establishRealTimeMonitoring();
}
```

In this React example, the code emphasizes the use of automated tools for regular scanning and auditing of IAM policies, coupled with real-time monitoring capabilities to swiftly identify and respond to potential security incidents.

In conclusion, IAM in the cloud forms the bedrock of a secure and well-managed cloud environment. By implementing RBAC, enforcing the principle of least privilege, automating identity lifecycle management, and establishing robust auditing and monitoring practices, organizations can fortify their IAM strategies. As the cloud computing landscape continues to evolve, adopting these IAM best practices ensures that organizations can navigate the complexities of identity and access management with confidence, safeguarding their digital assets and maintaining a resilient security stance.

Continuous Monitoring for Cloud Environments

The application of perpetual monitoring stands out as a crucial element in enhancing the security stance of organizations. As businesses progressively harness cloud environments to host their applications and data, the necessity for vigilant oversight and real-time insights into system activities becomes paramount. Continuous monitoring ensures the swift identification of potential threats, allowing for timely responses and strategies for mitigation.

To exemplify the concept of perpetual monitoring in a tangible manner, a React code snippet can be employed to showcase the implementation of real-time log analysis. Log analysis serves as a fundamental aspect of continuous monitoring, providing visibility into system events and potential security incidents.

```
// React code snippet for real-time log analysis in a cloud environment
function realTimeLogAnalysis() {
  // Set up log streaming from cloud services to a central analysis tool
  enableLogStreaming();

  // Implement real-time analysis of logs for detecting security anomalies
  analyzeLogsRealTime();
}
```

In this React example, the code depicts the configuration of log streaming from various cloud services to a centralized analysis tool. Real-time analysis of logs is then implemented, allowing for the swift detection of security anomalies.

Perpetual monitoring extends beyond log analysis and encompasses various aspects, including network traffic, system performance, and user activities. Utilizing React, organizations can represent the continuous surveillance of network traffic, emphasizing the significance of real-time monitoring to detect and respond to potential security threats.

```
// React code snippet for continuous surveillance of network traffic in a cloud
environment
function continuousNetworkSurveillance() {
  // Deploy network monitoring tools to capture real-time traffic data
  deployNetworkMonitoringTools();

  // Emphasize the importance of real-time monitoring for threat detection
  underscoreRealTimeMonitoring();
}
```

This React example emphasizes the deployment of network monitoring tools to capture real-time traffic data and underscores the critical role of continuous monitoring in threat detection.

Automated vulnerability assessments are integral to continuous monitoring practices, aiding organizations in proactively identifying and addressing potential security weaknesses. A React-based code snippet can showcase the implementation of automated vulnerability scans within a cloud environment.

```
// React code snippet for automated vulnerability
scanning in a cloud environment
function automateVulnerabilityScans() {
  // Integrate automated vulnerability scanning tools
into CI/CD pipelines
  integrateVulnerabilityScanning();

  // Schedule regular automated scans to identify and
remediate vulnerabilities
  scheduleAutomatedScans();
}
```

In this React example, the code highlights the integration of automated vulnerability scanning tools into continuous integration and continuous deployment (CI/CD) pipelines. Regular automated scans are scheduled to identify and remediate vulnerabilities, aligning with the proactive nature of continuous monitoring.

Continuous monitoring also involves the establishment of baselines for normal system behavior, enabling the detection of deviations that may indicate potential security threats. A

React code snippet can illustrate the creation of baseline profiles and the ongoing monitoring for anomalies.

```
// React code snippet for establishing baseline profiles
and monitoring for
anomalies
function establishBaselineAndMonitorAnomalies() {
  // Develop baseline profiles for normal system behavior
  createBaselineProfiles();

  // Continuously monitor system activities for
deviations from established baselines
  monitorForAnomalies();
}
```

This React example emphasizes the importance of developing baseline profiles for normal system behavior and the continuous monitoring of system activities to detect deviations.

In conclusion, perpetual monitoring in cloud environments is indispensable for maintaining a robust security posture. By incorporating real-time log analysis, continuous surveillance of network traffic, automated vulnerability assessments, and the establishment of baselines, organizations can effectively detect and respond to potential security threats. The utilization of React code snippets serves to concretize these concepts, making the implementation of continuous monitoring practices more tangible and actionable for security professionals in the dynamic field of cloud computing.

Chapter Nine

Incident Response and Cyber Forensics

Developing an Effective Incident Response Plan

Crafting a resilient incident response plan stands as a pivotal measure for organizations seeking to adeptly navigate and recover from security incidents. Such a plan acts as a strategic guidebook, offering a systematic approach to identifying, managing, and resolving security breaches.

A crucial facet of a potent incident response plan involves delineating explicit roles and responsibilities within the organization. By clearly defining the duties of those involved in incident response, organizations can ensure a well-coordinated and efficient response to security incidents. React code snippets can be employed to visually illustrate the assignment of responsibilities:

```
// React code snippet for delineating roles in incident response
function defineIncidentResponseRoles() {
  // Specify roles for incident responders, communication coordinators, and technical analysts
  const incidentResponderRole = specifyIncidentResponderRole();
  const communicationCoordinatorRole = specifyCommunicationCoordinatorRole();
```

```
  const technicalAnalystRole =
specifyTechnicalAnalystRole();

  // Allocate roles to relevant personnel
  allocateRole(incidentResponderRole, "Incident
Responder");
  allocateRole(communicationCoordinatorRole,
"Communication Coordinator");
  allocateRole(technicalAnalystRole, "Technical
Analyst");
}
```

This representation using React code showcases the articulation of roles such as incident responder, communication coordinator, and technical analyst, followed by the assignment of these roles to pertinent personnel.

Another integral facet of incident response planning involves the formulation of an incident classification system. React code snippets can serve to depict the implementation of a classification system categorizing incidents based on their severity and impact:

```
// React code snippet for incident classification in
incident response
function classifyIncidents() {
  // Implement an incident classification system based on
severity and impact
  const incidentSeverity = implementIncidentSeverity();
  const incidentImpact = implementIncidentImpact();

  // Categorize incidents using the established system
  const incidentClass =
categorizeIncident(incidentSeverity, incidentImpact);
}
```

This illustrative React example underscores the integration of an incident classification system that considers both severity and impact, providing a structured approach to sorting and prioritizing incidents.

Effective communication constitutes a cornerstone of successful incident response. React code snippets can visually demonstrate the integration of communication channels and tools to facilitate prompt and efficient communication during an incident:

```
// React code snippet for integrating communication tools
in incident response
function integrateCommunicationTools() {
  // Establish communication channels, such as chat
platforms and notification systems
  const chatPlatform = setCommunicationChannel("Chat
Platform");
  const notificationSystem =
setCommunicationChannel("Notification System");

  // Fuse tools for real-time collaboration and
information sharing
  fuseCollaborationTools(chatPlatform,
notificationSystem);
}
```

This React example places emphasis on the significance of communication tools like chat platforms and notification systems, highlighting their integration to enable real-time collaboration and information sharing.

Routine testing and refinement of the incident response plan are imperative to ensure its effectiveness. React code snippets can visually convey the execution of simulated incident scenarios and the subsequent assessment of the organization's response:

```jsx
// React code snippet for simulating incidents and
evaluating the response
function simulateAndEvaluateIncidents() {
  // Devise simulated incident scenarios to test the
response plan
  const simulatedIncidentScenarios =
createSimulatedScenarios();

  // Execute simulations and gauge the effectiveness of
the incident response
  conductSimulations(simulatedIncidentScenarios);
  evaluateResponseEffectiveness();
}
```

This React representation showcases the creation of simulated incident scenarios, the execution of simulations, and the evaluation of the incident response effectiveness.

To conclude, crafting an effective incident response plan is a crucial element of cybersecurity preparedness. By articulating clear roles, implementing an incident classification system, integrating communication tools, and regularly testing the plan through simulations, organizations can augment their ability to detect, respond to, and recover from security incidents. React code snippets offer a visual representation of these principles, making the development and implementation of an incident response plan more accessible and actionable for organizations in the dynamic and challenging sphere of cybersecurity.

Cyber Forensics Tools and Techniques

Effectively managing privacy settings and adhering to appropriate online conduct has emerged as a crucial facet of our interconnected lives. As we engage in diverse online platforms, spanning social media to collaborative workspaces, the significance of safeguarding personal information and engaging respectfully in the virtual space cannot be overstated.

A key element in preserving digital privacy involves skillfully navigating the privacy settings of various online platforms. Demonstrating practical aspects of securing personal information, React code snippets offer a visual representation of adjusting privacy configurations:

```
// React code snippet for customizing privacy settings on a social media platform
function customizePrivacySettings() {
  // Specify user preferences for profile visibility, post sharing, and contact details
  const profileVisibility = setProfileVisibility("Limited");
  const postSharing = setPostSharing("Friends Only");
  const contactDetails = setContactDetailsVisibility("Restricted");

  // Apply the chosen privacy settings
  applyPrivacySettings(profileVisibility, postSharing, contactDetails);
}
```

This React illustration showcases the tangible application of customizing privacy settings on a social media platform, encompassing choices related to profile visibility, post sharing, and contact information.

Furthermore, comprehending the ramifications of data sharing and adhering to responsible online behavior are integral aspects of digital citizenship. In collaborative tools like messaging apps and shared documents, exercising discretion and respecting others' privacy are fundamental. A React code snippet can depict a simplified example of responsible data sharing:

```
// React code snippet for responsible data sharing in a collaborative workspace
function shareDataPrudently() {
  // Establish a function to assess the sensitivity of shared data
  const checkDataSensitivity = (data) => {
    // Determine if data contains sensitive information
    return data.includes("confidential") ? "Sensitive" : "Non-sensitive";
  };

  // Share data selectively with necessary collaborators based on its sensitivity
  const sharedData = retrieveSharedData();
  const dataSensitivity = checkDataSensitivity(sharedData);

  if (dataSensitivity === "Sensitive") {
```

```
  Share sensitive data with specific users, such as
"Team Lead" and "Project Manager"
    shareWithSpecificUsers(sharedData, ["Team Lead",
"Project Manager"]);
  } else {
    Share non-sensitive data with the entire team
    shareWithTeam(sharedData);
  }
}
```

In this React instance, the code encourages judicious data sharing by evaluating the sensitivity of shared data and then sharing it selectively with the appropriate collaborators.

Moreover, online etiquette extends beyond data sharing to encompass considerate communication and behavior. React code can underscore the importance of maintaining a positive online presence:

```
// React code snippet for fostering positive online
etiquette
function exhibitOnlineEtiquette() {
  // Promote courteous and constructive communication
  const comment = "Commendable effort on the project!";
  const positiveResponse = respondPositively(comment);

  // Establish guidelines for offering constructive
feedback and managing disagreements
```

```
  const constructiveFeedback =
provideConstructiveFeedback("Consider exploring
alternative approaches.");

  // Implement a mechanism to report inappropriate
behavior
  const reportInappropriateBehavior =
reportUser("Unprofessional conduct");

  // Display a notification acknowledging positive online
conduct
  displayNotification(positiveResponse, "success");
}
```

This React representation emphasizes code-based encouragement for positive online etiquette, covering aspects like polite communication, constructive feedback, and mechanisms to report inappropriate behavior.

In conclusion, as we navigate the digital landscape, the nuanced management of privacy settings and adherence to respectful online conduct remain pivotal. React code snippets offer a tangible way to illustrate the practical aspects of adjusting privacy configurations and promoting responsible online behavior. Integrating these practices into our digital interactions contributes to a more secure and considerate online environment.

Post-Incident Analysis and Improvement

Following a cybersecurity incident, a comprehensive analysis of the aftermath and the subsequent implementation of enhancements based on the findings play pivotal roles in fortifying the security stance. This process goes beyond merely discerning the root causes of the issue; it involves strengthening defenses and mitigating potential risks in the future.

An essential facet of post-incident analysis involves scrutinizing the attack vector and pinpointing vulnerabilities that may have been exploited. In a React environment, a code snippet can visually elucidate the process of parsing log files to trace the steps of an intrusion:

```
// React code snippet for the systematic parsing of log files during post
incident analysis
function analyzeLogsForInsights() {
  // Extract and scrutinize log files to identify any unusual activities
  const logData = fetchLogData();
  const identifiedAnomalies = pinpointAnomalies(logData);

  // Compile a comprehensive report summarizing the attack vector and exploited vulnerabilities
  const attackVectorSummary = createAttackVectorSummary(identifiedAnomalies);
  presentFindings(attackVectorSummary);
}
```

This React example effectively demonstrates the practical application of parsing log files to extract pertinent information during the post-incident analysis. It underscores the importance of methodically examining logs to gain insights into the intricacies of the attack.

Additionally, a pivotal aspect of the improvement process post-incident involves the application of patches or updates to rectify vulnerabilities. React code can showcase the deployment of security patches:

```
// React code snippet illustrating the deployment of security patches post incident analysis
function applySecurityUpdates() {
  // Identify vulnerabilities identified in the incident analysis
  const identifiedWeaknesses = assessIncidentAndRecognizeWeaknesses();

  // Formulate and implement security patches to address the identified vulnerabilities
  const securityPatches = createSecurityPatches(identifiedWeaknesses);
  implementPatches(securityPatches);
}
```

This React representation accentuates the practical execution of deploying security patches following the analysis of an incident. It emphasizes the urgency of taking swift action to rectify vulnerabilities and reinforce the security stance.

Moreover, post-incident analysis encompasses the reassessment of incident response procedures. React code can be employed to demonstrate the refinement of incident response processes:

```
// React code snippet illustrating the enhancement of incident response
procedures
function refineIncidentResponsePlans() {
  // Scrutinize incident response procedures and pinpoint areas that warrant improvement
  const incidentResponsePlans = evaluateIncidentResponsePlans();
  const identifiedEnhancementAreas = recognizeAreasForImprovement(incidentResponsePlans);

  // Integrate changes to elevate the effectiveness of incident response
  implementAdjustments(identifiedEnhancementAreas);
}
```

This React example elucidates the practical steps involved in reviewing incident response procedures and making necessary alterations to augment the overall efficacy of the response plan.

The process of post-incident analysis and improvement constitutes indispensable elements in the ongoing refinement of an organization's cybersecurity posture. React code snippets offer a tangible means of illustrating the practical aspects of parsing log files, deploying security patches, and refining incident response procedures. By seamlessly integrating these practices into the cybersecurity strategy, organizations can not only recover from incidents but also bolster their defenses against potential threats.

Legal and Ethical Considerations in Incident Response

Navigating the intricate landscape of incident response involves a delicate balance of technical acumen and an astute awareness of the legal and ethical facets inherent in this crucial cybersecurity practice. As organizations grapple with the consequences of security incidents, they must adeptly navigate a framework that attends to legal obligations and upholds ethical standards.

In the context of incident response, React code serves as a practical illustration of how legal considerations seamlessly integrate into the process. For instance, when addressing personally identifiable information (PII) post a data breach, compliance with data protection laws becomes paramount. Here's a simplified React code snippet that underscores the significance of adherence:

```
// React code snippet illustrating legal compliance in managing PII during
incident response
function manageDataBreach(dataBreachDetails) {
  // Scrutinize the involvement of PII
  const hasPII = checkForPII(dataBreachDetails);
```

```
// Ensure alignment with data protection laws
if (hasPII) {
  const legalCompliance =
ensureDataProtectionCompliance(dataBreachDetails);
  reportLegalStatus(legalCompliance);
}

// Proceed with incident response actions
  initiateResponseActions(dataBreachDetails);
}
```

This React instance encapsulates the idea of weaving legal compliance into incident response, particularly when handling PII. It illustrates the necessity of evaluating and reporting on the legal status before proceeding with response actions.

Ethical considerations stand as an equally integral component of incident response efforts. React code vividly portrays the ethical imperative of transparency and communication with affected parties during a security incident:

```
// React code snippet highlighting ethical communication
during incident response
function communicateWithAffectedParties(incidentDetails)
{
  // Evaluate the impact of the incident on stakeholders
  const impactOnStakeholders =
assessImpactOnStakeholders(incidentDetails);

  // Ethically communicate the incident and its
ramifications
  if (impactOnStakeholders) {
```

```
    ethicallyCommunicateIncident(incidentDetails,
impactOnStakeholders);
  }

  // Proceed with incident response actions
  continueWithResponseActions(incidentDetails);
}
```

This React demonstration underscores the ethical necessity of transparently communicating with stakeholders about the incident's impact before progressing with response actions.

Moreover, incident response teams must factor in legal frameworks dictating the reporting of specific incidents. React code vividly portrays the adherence to regulatory requirements:

```
// React code snippet showcasing adherence to legal
reporting requirements
function complyWithRegulatoryObligations(incidentDetails)
{
  // Identify regulatory obligations linked to the
incident
  const regulatoryObligations =
identifyRegulatoryObligations(incidentDetails);

  // Adhere to legal reporting requirements
  if (regulatoryObligations) {
    ensureLegalReporting(regulatoryObligations);
```

```
}
// Proceed with incident response actions
handleIncidentAppropriately(incidentDetails);
}
```

This React example brings to light the practical amalgamation of legal considerations into incident response by ensuring conformity with regulatory reporting requirements.

The successful execution of incident response transcends technical expertise; it mandates a holistic grasp of the legal and ethical dimensions. React code snippets offer a tangible representation of how legal compliance and ethical communication seamlessly coalesce within incident response processes. By harmonizing technical acumen with legal and ethical considerations, organizations can navigate the aftermath of security incidents with meticulous diligence and responsibility.

Chapter Ten

Securing IoT Devices

Risks Associated with IoT Devices

The surge in Internet of Things (IoT) devices not only introduces various conveniences but also brings forth a spectrum of security challenges that require meticulous attention. As organizations and individuals seamlessly integrate IoT devices into their daily routines, comprehending and addressing these challenges becomes imperative to ensure a robust cybersecurity posture.

When exploring the technical facets, React code snippets can vividly portray the potential risks linked with IoT devices. For instance, insecure communication protocols may render IoT devices vulnerable to eavesdropping and data interception. The following React code exemplifies a common oversight:

```
// React code illustrating insecure communication in an IoT device
function insecureCommunication(deviceEndpoint, sensitiveData) {
  // Transmitting data without encryption
  fetch(`http://${deviceEndpoint}/transmitData`, {
    method: 'POST',
    body: JSON.stringify({ data: sensitiveData }),
    headers: {
      'Content-Type': 'application/json',
    },
```

```
});
}
```

This React example showcases a scenario where sensitive data is transmitted without encryption, exposing it to potential interception. It underscores the risk associated with inadequate security measures in communication protocols.

Another prevalent risk involves the insufficient implementation of device authentication. React code can effectively highlight the vulnerability associated with weak authentication mechanisms:

```
// React code illustrating weak device authentication
function weakAuthentication(deviceCredentials) {
  // Authenticating the device with inadequate credentials
  authenticateDevice(deviceCredentials);
}
```

This React snippet symbolizes a situation where a device is authenticated with weak credentials, making it susceptible to unauthorized access. It accentuates the importance of robust authentication mechanisms in mitigating IoT security risks.

Furthermore, insecure device firmware and software pose substantial threats. React code can visually depict the potential consequences of outdated or vulnerable firmware:

```
// React code illustrating the risk of insecure firmware
function insecureFirmwareUpdate(deviceFirmware) {
  // Attempting to update device firmware with a
vulnerable version
  updateDeviceFirmware(deviceFirmware);
}
```

In this React instance, the attempt to update the device firmware with a version known to have vulnerabilities underscores the criticality of regularly patching and securing IoT device software.

Additionally, the interconnected nature of IoT devices creates a cascading effect, where a compromise in one device can lead to a domino effect on the entire network. React code can portray the interconnected vulnerabilities:

```
// React code illustrating the interconnected
vulnerabilities of IoT devices
function interconnectedVulnerabilities(compromisedDevice)
{
  // Exploiting one compromised device to infiltrate the
entire network
  exploitInterconnectedDevices(compromisedDevice);
}
```

This React example showcases the potential exploitation of interconnected vulnerabilities, emphasizing the need for robust network segmentation and isolation to contain potential breaches.

In conclusion, the integration of IoT devices into our interconnected world presents a spectrum of security challenges that demand proactive measures. React code snippets serve as a tangible means to illustrate these risks, from insecure communication protocols to weak authentication mechanisms. Recognizing these vulnerabilities is the initial step toward implementing comprehensive security strategies, encompassing encryption, strong authentication, regular software updates, and thoughtful network architecture to ensure the resilience of IoT ecosystems against evolving cyber threats.

Implementing Security Controls for IoT

Securing Internet of Things (IoT) devices has become a crucial task, given their widespread integration into our daily lives. The implementation of robust security controls for IoT is essential to mitigate potential risks and protect sensitive data. This requires a comprehensive approach that includes encryption, secure communication protocols, and strict access controls.

One crucial aspect of implementing security controls for IoT lies in adopting robust encryption practices. React code snippets can effectively illustrate the importance of encrypting data transmitted between IoT devices and backend servers:

```
// React code illustrating encrypted data transmission in
IoT
function ensureSecureDataTransmission(deviceEndpoint,
sensitiveData) {
  // Transmitting data with encryption
  fetch(`https://${deviceEndpoint}/transmitData`, {
    method: 'POST',
    body: encryptData(sensitiveData),
    headers: {
      'Content-Type': 'application/json',
    },
  });
}

// Encryption function for sensitive data
function encryptData(data) {
  // Implement encryption logic here
  // Example: Using a hypothetical encryption library
  return encryptionLibrary.encrypt(data);
}
```

This React example demonstrates the implementation of encrypted data transmission, emphasizing the significance of securing the communication channel between IoT devices and backend services.

Additionally, enforcing secure communication protocols is paramount in IoT security. React code can visually represent the vulnerability associated with using insecure protocols:

```js
// React code illustrating secure communication protocol
// in IoT
function ensureSecureCommunication(deviceEndpoint,
sensitiveData) {
  // Transmitting data with HTTPS
  fetch(`https://${deviceEndpoint}/transmitData`, {
    method: 'POST',
    body: JSON.stringify({ data: sensitiveData }),
    headers: {
      'Content-Type': 'application/json',
    },
  });
}

// React code illustrating insecure communication
// protocol in IoT
function useInsecureCommunication(deviceEndpoint,
sensitiveData) {
  // Transmitting data with HTTP (insecure)
  fetch(`http://${deviceEndpoint}/transmitData`, {
    method: 'POST',
    body: JSON.stringify({ data: sensitiveData }),
    headers: {
      'Content-Type': 'application/json',
    },
  });
}
```

This React snippet showcases the importance of using secure communication protocols like HTTPS instead of insecure alternatives like HTTP, which could expose data to potential interception.

Furthermore, implementing stringent access controls is vital to prevent unauthorized access to IoT devices. React code can depict the difference between a device with robust access controls and one with lax security:

```
// React code illustrating robust access controls in IoT
function implementAccessControls(deviceCredentials, sensitiveOperation) {
  // Checking device credentials before allowing sensitive operation
  if (validateCredentials(deviceCredentials)) {
    performSensitiveOperation(sensitiveOperation);
  } else {
    // Handle unauthorized access
    handleUnauthorizedAccess();
  }
}

// React code illustrating lax access controls in IoT
function neglectAccessControls(deviceCredentials, sensitiveOperation) {
  // Allowing sensitive operation without proper credential validation
  performSensitiveOperation(sensitiveOperation);
}
```

This React example emphasizes the necessity of enforcing access controls by validating device credentials before permitting sensitive operations, reducing the risk of unauthorized access.

In conclusion, securing IoT devices involves a multifaceted approach, and the implementation of security controls is a pivotal aspect. React code snippets provide a tangible representation of the importance of encryption, secure communication protocols, and stringent access controls in fortifying IoT security. Embracing these practices is essential to navigate the complex landscape of IoT security challenges and ensure the integrity and confidentiality of data in an interconnected world.

IoT Device Lifecycle Security

Ensuring the security of Internet of Things (IoT) devices throughout their lifecycle remains a top priority. The IoT device journey spans from inception and design to deployment and eventual decommissioning, presenting a series of challenges that demand meticulous attention to security details. Let's explore key considerations and best practices in securing the IoT device lifecycle, using React code snippets to exemplify practical implementation.

1.Secure Bootstrapping: At the start of an IoT device's lifecycle, establishing secure bootstrapping is crucial to ensure the device starts in a known secure state. React code can illustrate the initiation of secure bootstrapping:

```
// React code illustrating secure bootstrapping in IoT
device
function initiateSecureBoot(deviceID) {
  // Perform secure bootstrapping operations
  establishTrustedConnection(deviceID);
  validateFirmwareIntegrity();
  // Continue device initialization
  initializeDevice();
}
```

This React snippet showcases the initiation of secure bootstrapping, including steps like establishing a trusted connection and validating firmware integrity.

2. Firmware Integrity Checks: Throughout the operational phase of the IoT device, regular checks to ensure the integrity of the firmware are essential. React code can portray the implementation of firmware integrity checks:

```
// React code illustrating firmware integrity checks in
IoT device
function checkFirmwareIntegrity() {
  // Retrieve firmware from secure source
  const firmware = retrieveSecureFirmware();

  // Validate firmware integrity
  if (validateIntegrity(firmware)) {
    // Firmware is intact, proceed with update or
operation
```

```
    performSecureOperation();
} else {
    // Handle compromised firmware
    handleCompromisedFirmware();
}
}
```

This React example demonstrates the importance of validating firmware integrity before executing any secure operation, mitigating the risk of compromised firmware.

3. Over-the-Air (OTA) Updates Security: Enabling secure Over-the-Air (OTA) updates is critical for keeping IoT devices resilient against emerging threats. React code can visualize the secure implementation of OTA updates:

```
// React code illustrating secure OTA update in IoT device
function secureOTAUpdate(deviceID, updatedFirmware) {
    // Validate the authenticity of the update
    if (validateUpdateAuthenticity(updatedFirmware)) {
        // Apply the OTA update securely
        applyOTAUpdate(deviceID, updatedFirmware);
    } else {
        // Handle unauthorized or compromised updates
        handleUnauthorizedUpdate();
    }
}
```

This React snippet emphasizes the necessity of validating the authenticity of OTA updates before applying them to prevent unauthorized or compromised updates.

4. End-of-Life (EOL) Considerations: When an IoT device reaches the end of its operational life, secure decommissioning is essential to prevent security loopholes. React code can portray secure end-of-life considerations:

```
// React code illustrating secure end-of-life process in IoT device
function decommissionDevice(deviceID) {
  // Securely wipe sensitive data
  eraseSensitiveData(deviceID);
  // Notify central management system of decommissioning
  notifyDecommission(deviceID);
  // Physically secure the device for disposal
  secureDisposal(deviceID);
}
```

This React example underscores the importance of securely wiping sensitive data, notifying central systems, and physically securing the device during decommissioning.

In conclusion, safeguarding the IoT device lifecycle demands a comprehensive approach encompassing secure bootstrapping, firmware integrity checks, secure OTA updates, and diligent end-of-life considerations. React code snippets offer a tangible representation of these security measures, reinforcing the practical implementation of robust security practices throughout the diverse phases of an IoT device's lifecycle. By embracing these security considerations, organizations can enhance the overall security posture of their IoT deployments and navigate the challenges inherent in the dynamic landscape of IoT security.

The Intersection of IoT and Industrial Control Systems (ICS) Security

The interplay between Internet of Things (IoT) and Industrial Control Systems (ICS) introduces a fresh layer to the intricacies of security. As industries progressively intertwine IoT devices into operational processes, the convergence with ICS amplifies both the gains in efficiency and the considerations for security. Exploring the dynamic relationship between IoT and ICS security reveals a multifaceted ecosystem that demands meticulous attention and a strategic approach. Let's delve into crucial aspects, employing React code snippets where applicable to illustrate practical insights.

1.Integration Challenges: The amalgamation of IoT and ICS introduces integration challenges, particularly when various devices necessitate seamless communication. React code can offer a simplified representation of data exchange between an IoT device and an ICS system:

```
// React code illustrating data exchange between IoT device and ICS
function sendDataToICS(sensorData) {
  // Validate and format data
  const formattedData = validateAndFormat(sensorData);
  // Dispatch data to ICS for processing
```

```
  sendToICS(formattedData);
}
```

This React snippet illustrates the streamlined data exchange process between an IoT sensor and an ICS system, underscoring the importance of proper validation and formatting.

2. Security Protocols and Standards: Ensuring standardized security protocols across both IoT and ICS components is crucial. React code can exemplify the implementation of secure communication:

```
// React code illustrating secure communication between IoT and ICS
function secureCommunication(deviceID, command) {
  // Authenticate device with ICS
  authenticateWithICS(deviceID);

  // Transmit secure command to the device
  sendSecureCommand(deviceID, command);
}
```

This React example underscores the significance of device authentication and secure command transmission within the context of IoT-ICS integration.

3. Edge Computing in Industrial Environments: The deployment of edge computing in industrial settings, facilitated by IoT devices, introduces efficiency but also poses security considerations. React code can showcase the local processing capabilities at the edge:

```
// React code illustrating edge computing in an
industrial setting
function processAtEdge(data) {
  // Implement local processing logic
  deriveLocalInsights(data);

  // Transmit processed data to central ICS
  relayToICS(data);
}
```

This React snippet illustrates the local processing capabilities at the edge, balancing the advantages of edge computing with the need to transmit relevant data to the central ICS.

4. Threats and Vulnerabilities: The intersection of IoT and ICS amplifies potential threats and vulnerabilities. React code can visualize a simple representation of a security monitoring system:

```
// React code illustrating a security monitoring system
for IoT-ICS
function monitorSecurityThreats() {
  // Continuously observe for security threats
  const threatDetected = watchForThreats();

  // Initiate preventive measures if a threat is detected
```

```
if (threatDetected) {
    implementPreventiveActions();
}
}
```

This React example emphasizes the ongoing monitoring for security threats in an IoT-ICS environment, incorporating a proactive response mechanism.

So, the intersection of IoT and ICS introduces innovation and efficiency into industrial processes but demands a meticulous approach to security. React code snippets provide a tangible representation of key considerations, from data exchange and secure communication to edge computing and threat monitoring. By addressing challenges strategically, industries can harness the benefits of IoT-ICS integration while fortifying their cybersecurity defenses in this dynamic technological landscape.

Chapter Eleven

Emerging Technologies and Future Trends

Exploring AI and Machine Learning in Cybersecurity

The collaboration between Artificial Intelligence (AI) and Machine Learning (ML) stands out as a dynamic force reshaping traditional security approaches with adaptable and forward-thinking capabilities. This exploration delves into the symbiotic relationship between AI, ML, and cybersecurity, shedding light on their collaborative role in strengthening digital defenses. Practical implementations and insights will be illustrated through React code snippets throughout this discussion.

1.Enhanced Threat Detection and Analysis: AI and ML significantly contribute to improving threat detection and analysis, providing a proactive defense against evolving cyber threats. The following React code snippet offers a simplified representation of an AI-driven threat detection mechanism:

```
// React code illustrating AI-driven threat detection
function detectThreats(data) {
  // Use machine learning models for threat analysis
  const threatLevel = analyzeWithML(data);

  // Initiate suitable actions based on the threat level
  respondToThreat(threatLevel);
}
```

This React example showcases the seamless integration of ML models to scrutinize incoming data and trigger tailored responses based on the identified threat level.

2. Identification of Unusual Patterns in Network Traffic: AI and ML play a crucial role in recognizing anomalies within network traffic, indicating potential security incidents. The following React code provides a glimpse into an anomaly detection system:

```
// React code illustrating anomaly detection in network traffic
function monitorNetworkTraffic() {
  // Implement machine learning algorithms for anomaly detection
  identifyAnomalies();

  // Manage and respond to identified anomalies
  handleAnomalies();
}
```

This React snippet emphasizes the application of ML algorithms to consistently monitor network traffic and identify unusual patterns indicative of potential security threats.

3. Proactive Security Measures: Machine Learning facilitates the creation of predictive models that anticipate and prevent security breaches. The following React code snippet demonstrates a simplified predictive security measure:

```
// React code illustrating predictive security measures
function predictSecurityEvents(data) {
  // Train ML models to predict potential security events
  const prediction = trainAndPredict(data);

  // Implement preventive actions based on the prediction
  takePreventiveMeasures(prediction);
}
```

This React example illustrates the training of ML models to forecast security events, allowing for the implementation of proactive measures to mitigate potential risks.

4. User Authentication Behavioral Analysis: AI and ML excel in behavioral analysis, enhancing user authentication processes. The following React code showcases a behavioral authentication system:

```
// React code illustrating behavioral analysis for user
authentication
function authenticateUserBehavior(userInput) {
  // Utilize ML to analyze user behavior patterns
  analyzeBehavior(userInput);

  // Grant or deny authentication based on the analysis
  authenticateBasedOnBehavior();
}
```

This React snippet highlights the incorporation of ML for real-time analysis of user behavior, influencing authentication decisions.

The collaboration between AI, ML, and cybersecurity signifies a paradigm shift in the approach to safeguarding digital assets. React code snippets have provided tangible representations of AI and ML applications in threat detection, anomaly monitoring, predictive security measures, and behavioral analysis. As these technologies continue to evolve, their integration offers a powerful arsenal for organizations seeking resilient cybersecurity solutions in the dynamic landscape of digital security.

Quantum Computing and its Implications for Security

The arrival of quantum computing initiates a transformative shift with profound consequences for the cybersecurity sector. This exploration delves into the complexities of quantum computing and its potential impacts on security protocols, avoiding elaborate metaphors or technical jargon. To facilitate a clearer understanding, snippets of React code will be incorporated to illustrate key concepts.

1. Quantum Supremacy and Shor's Algorithm: Quantum supremacy, a term indicating the point at which quantum computers surpass the capabilities of classical computers, is a notable milestone. Shor's algorithm, a quantum algorithm designed for integer factorization, presents a substantial threat to widely-used cryptographic schemes. The following React code demonstrates a simplified version of Shor's algorithm:

```
// React code illustrating a simplified version of Shor's algorithm
function shorsAlgorithm(factorizableNumber) {
  // Quantum operations for integer factorization
  const factors = quantumFactorization(factorizableNumber);

  // Utilize the obtained factors to compromise classical cryptography
  compromiseCryptography(factors);
}
```

This React example provides a basic representation of the quantum operations involved in Shor's algorithm, which, when scaled on quantum computers, could compromise the security of widely-used cryptographic systems.

2. Quantum Key Distribution (QKD): As quantum computing poses a threat to classical cryptography, Quantum Key Distribution (QKD) emerges as a potential solution. QKD leverages the principles of quantum mechanics to secure communication channels. The following React code snippet showcases a simplified QKD process:

```
// React code illustrating a simplified Quantum Key
Distribution process
function quantumKeyDistribution() {
  // Quantum entanglement and key exchange
  const quantumEntanglement = createEntangledParticles();
  const secureKey =
exchangeQuantumKey(quantumEntanglement);

  // Use the secure key for encrypted communication
  initiateSecureCommunication(secureKey);
}
```

This React example symbolizes the principles of quantum entanglement and secure key exchange integral to Quantum Key Distribution, ensuring the confidentiality of communication.

3. Post-Quantum Cryptography: Acknowledging the vulnerability of current cryptographic methods to quantum attacks, the field of post-quantum cryptography aims to develop algorithms resistant to quantum threats. The following React code depicts the transition to post-quantum cryptographic algorithms:

```
// React code illustrating the transition to post-quantum
cryptography
function postQuantumCryptography(data) {
  // Utilize cryptographic algorithms resistant to
quantum attacks
  const encryptedData = postQuantumEncrypt(data);

  // Safeguard communication against quantum threats
  ensureQuantumResistantCommunication(encryptedData);
}
```

This React snippet signifies the incorporation of post-quantum cryptographic algorithms to secure data in a quantum-threatened environment.

4. Impact on Blockchain Technology: Quantum computing also has implications for blockchain technology, particularly regarding the security of public-key cryptography used in blockchain networks. The following React code snippet captures the essence of potential threats to blockchain security

```
// React code illustrating the potential impact of
quantum computing on
blockchain
function quantumImpactOnBlockchain() {
  // Quantum algorithms compromising public-key
cryptography
  const quantumThreats =
analyzeBlockchainVulnerabilities();
```

```
// Implement countermeasures to secure blockchain
networks
  implementBlockchainSecurityMeasures(quantumThreats);
}
```

This React example highlights the need for proactive security measures in blockchain networks to counter potential threats posed by quantum computing.

In conclusion, the rise of quantum computing introduces both challenges and opportunities for the cybersecurity sector. This exploration, free from metaphorical expressions, has utilized React code snippets to elucidate key concepts such as quantum supremacy, Shor's algorithm, Quantum Key Distribution, post-quantum cryptography, and the impact on blockchain technology. Staying informed about these developments is crucial for maintaining robust security measures in the evolving landscape of digital security.

Biometric Security Advancements

Advancements in biometric security emerge as a pivotal means to enhance authentication methods and fortify digital systems. This exploration delves into the technical aspects of biometric security without relying on metaphorical expressions. To elucidate key concepts, React code snippets will be integrated where relevant.

1. Evolution of Biometric Modalities: Biometric security has undergone a notable shift in modalities, expanding beyond traditional fingerprint recognition. Facial recognition, iris scanning, voice recognition, and behavioral biometrics have gained prominence. The following React code exemplifies a simplified facial recognition process:

```
// React code illustrating a basic facial recognition
process
function facialRecognition(image) {
  // Utilize facial recognition algorithms for identity
verification
  const identityVerified =
performFacialRecognition(image);

  // Grant access upon successful identity verification
  grantAccess(identityVerified);
}
```

This React example represents the application of facial recognition algorithms, showcasing the shift towards diverse biometric modalities.

2. Multifactor Authentication Integration: Biometric security often integrates into multifactor authentication (MFA) systems, enhancing overall security. Combining biometrics with traditional factors like passwords strengthens access control. The React code snippet below depicts a simplified MFA process:

```
// React code illustrating a basic multifactor
authentication process
function multifactorAuthentication(biometricData,
password) {
  // Verify biometric data and validate password
  const biometricVerified =
verifyBiometricData(biometricData);
  const passwordValidated = validatePassword(password);

  // Grant access if both factors are successfully
validated
  grantAccess(biometricVerified && passwordValidated);
}
```

This React example illustrates the amalgamation of biometric verification and password validation in a multifactor authentication setup.

3. Continuous Authentication Paradigm: Continuous authentication, a paradigm shift in biometric security, involves ongoing verification during a user's session. Behavioral biometrics, such as keystroke dynamics or mouse movement, play a crucial role. The following React snippet demonstrates a simplified continuous authentication scenario:

```
// React code illustrating a basic continuous
authentication scenario
function continuousAuthentication(keystrokePattern,
mouseMovement) {
```

```
// Continuously verify behavioral biometrics throughout the user's session
  const behavioralBiometricsVerified = verifyBehavioralBiometrics(keystrokePattern, mouseMovement);

  // Maintain secure access based on continuous authentication
  maintainSecureSession(behavioralBiometricsVerified);
}
```

This React example symbolizes the continuous verification of behavioral biometrics to ensure secure user sessions.

4. Robustness Against Spoofing Attempts: As biometric systems advance, robustness against spoofing attempts becomes paramount. Techniques like liveness detection are implemented to distinguish between live biometric samples and replicas. The React code below provides a simplistic representation:

```
// React code illustrating a basic liveness detection process
function livenessDetection(biometricSample) {
  // Implement liveness detection algorithms to discern live samples from replicas
  const isLiveSample = detectLiveness(biometricSample);
```

```
// Proceed with authentication if the sample is
determined to be live
  authenticate(isLiveSample);
}
```

This React snippet showcases the application of liveness detection algorithms to enhance biometric security by preventing spoofing.

5. Privacy Concerns and Ethical Considerations: Amidst technological progress, addressing privacy concerns and ethical considerations is imperative. Biometric data storage and processing must adhere to stringent privacy standards. The React code snippet below symbolizes a privacy-centric approach in biometric data handling:

```
// React code illustrating a privacy-centric approach in
biometric data handling
function handleBiometricData(biometricData) {
  // Ensure adherence to privacy standards while
processing biometric data
  const processedData =
handleBiometricPrivacy(biometricData);

  // Proceed with secure data storage and processing
  secureBiometricDataStorage(processedData);
}
```

This React example emphasizes the importance of privacy-centric practices in the storage and processing of biometric data.

In conclusion, advancements in biometric security significantly contribute to the ever-changing landscape of cybersecurity. This exploration, free from metaphorical expressions, utilizes React code snippets to elucidate key concepts, including the evolution of biometric modalities, multifactor authentication integration, the continuous authentication paradigm, robustness against spoofing, and the consideration of privacy and ethics. Embracing these advancements is crucial for organizations striving to establish a resilient cybersecurity defense.

The Role of Automation in Cyber Defense

the pivotal role of automation in fortifying cyber defenses is evident. Automation serves as a central element in building resilient security postures, enabling organizations to efficiently detect, respond to, and mitigate threats. This exploration delves into the technical aspects of automation without relying on figurative expressions. To elucidate key concepts, React code snippets will be seamlessly integrated where applicable.

1.Automated Threat Detection: Automated mechanisms play a crucial role in swiftly identifying potential threats within a network. Leveraging React, let's exemplify a simplified scenario:

```
function detectThreats(networkTraffic) {
  const threatsDetected =
automatedThreatDetection(networkTraffic);
  respondToThreats(threatsDetected);
}
```

This React example illustrates the application of automated algorithms in detecting potential threats within network traffic.

2. Incident Response Automation: Automation streamlines incident response workflows, ensuring rapid and efficient reactions to security incidents. A React code snippet can depict a basic incident response automation process:

```
function automateIncidentResponse(incidentDetails) {
  const automatedResponse =
executeAutomatedIncidentResponse(incidentDetails);
  logAutomatedResponse(automatedResponse);
}
```

This React example showcases the integration of automated workflows in incident response, facilitating timely reactions to security incidents.

3. Patch Management Automation: Automated patch management is essential for promptly addressing vulnerabilities and maintaining system security. React code can portray a straightforward patch management automation scenario:

```
function automatePatchManagement(systems, vulnerabilities) {
  const automatedPatchApplication = applyAutomatedPatches(systems, vulnerabilities);
  logPatchManagement(automatedPatchApplication);
}
```

This React snippet demonstrates the automated identification and application of patches to enhance system security.

4.Continuous Monitoring and Automated Alerts: Automation enables continuous monitoring of systems, coupled with the automated generation of alerts upon detecting anomalies. A React code example can showcase this continuous monitoring process:

```
function continuousMonitoring(systemMetrics) {
  const anomaliesDetected = monitorAndDetectAnomalies(systemMetrics);
  generateAutomatedAlerts(anomaliesDetected);
}
```

This React example highlights the integration of automation in continuous monitoring processes, enhancing the ability to detect and respond to anomalies promptly.

5. Automated Security Policy Enforcement: Automated enforcement of security policies ensures consistency and adherence to predefined standards. React code can represent a basic scenario of automated security policy enforcement:

```
function enforceSecurityPolicy(userActions, securityPolicy) {
  const policyViolations = evaluateAndEnforcePolicy(userActions, securityPolicy);
  respondToPolicyViolations(policyViolations);
}
```

This React snippet showcases the automated evaluation and enforcement of security policies to maintain a secure environment.

Automation stands as a cornerstone in cyber defense, offering unparalleled efficiency in identifying, responding to, and mitigating cyber threats. This exploration, void of metaphorical expressions, employs React code snippets to elucidate key automation concepts, including threat detection, incident response, patch management, continuous monitoring, and security policy enforcement. Embracing automation is imperative for organizations aiming to establish robust cybersecurity defenses in the face of evolving cyber threats.

Conclusions

Concluding our in-depth exploration into cybersecurity for those at an intermediate level, it's crucial to reflect on the diverse aspects we've covered. This guide isn't merely a compilation of technical insights; it's designed to empower professionals as they navigate the complex and dynamic challenges of securing digital environments.

Our exploration began by understanding prevalent cyber threats and recognizing the pivotal role of threat intelligence in strengthening defense mechanisms. From establishing foundational principles in network security to diving into advanced endpoint protection, we've laid a strong groundwork for comprehending the intricacies of the digital age.

The importance of secure coding practices became apparent as we delved into software development lifecycles and meticulous code review practices. These efforts aimed to fortify our software against potential vulnerabilities and ensure its robustness.

The journey of cybersecurity professionals extends beyond technical proficiency. We've become architects of trust, stewards of digital integrity, and guardians of a future where information flows securely. Each chapter in this guide has contributed to shaping us into custodians of a digital landscape that demands our unwavering vigilance.

The challenges encountered on our path were formidable, yet they served as crucibles, forging our resolve to protect the digital environments we inhabit. The delicate balance between security and user experience became evident, emphasizing the importance of seamlessly integrating secure systems into the daily lives of users.

Standing at the intersection of knowledge and experience, the question arises: What lies ahead? The digital landscape is dynamic, with threats mutating and technology evolving. Our response must be equally dynamic, rooted in a commitment to continuous improvement.

For those overseeing software development, integrating security into the Software Development Lifecycle (SDLC) is not a perfunctory task; it is a philosophy. Consider a scenario where a web application, a cornerstone of modern development, becomes a battleground between security and innovation:

In the pursuit of secure coding practices, a simple validation step ensures the application becomes a stronghold of access control, impervious to unauthorized access.

Gazing into the future, the horizon is both promising and challenging. Emerging technologies like Artificial Intelligence (AI) and Machine Learning (ML) beckon, offering unparalleled insights into threat detection and mitigation. Yet, they come with their own set of ethical considerations, as biases in algorithms and the ethical use of AI become pivotal points of discourse.

Quantum computing, with its potential to unravel traditional cryptographic algorithms, presents a formidable challenge. Our cryptographic protocols must evolve, embracing post-quantum cryptography to secure our digital transactions in a quantum-powered era.

Biometric security, once a concept relegated to science fiction, is rapidly becoming a tangible reality. The fusion of biology and technology introduces a paradigm shift, demanding that we recalibrate our understanding of identity and access management.

Automation, a trusted ally in the quest for efficiency, assumes a more pronounced role in cyber defense. From threat detection to incident response, the marriage of human expertise and machine efficiency becomes the linchpin of future cybersecurity frameworks.

As we conclude this comprehensive guide, it's important to recognize that cybersecurity for those at an intermediate level is not just about knowledge acquisition; it's a manifesto for empowerment. Armed with knowledge, fortified by experience, and driven by an unyielding commitment to digital integrity, we step into the future, not as mere observers but as architects of a secure, connected reality.

The path ahead may be winding, but with each step, we carve a secure, resilient future for the digital environments we call home.

Printed in Great Britain
by Amazon